Allan Shepard

Ahimsa
The Timeless Wisdom of Jainism

Original Title: Ahimsa - A Sabedoria Atemporal do Jainismo

Copyright © 2025, published by Luiz Antonio dos Santos ME.
This book is a non-fiction work that explores the principles and philosophy of Jainism, focusing on the concept of Ahimsa (non-violence) as a fundamental ethical and spiritual practice. Through a comprehensive approach, the author provides historical insights, ethical perspectives, and practical applications of Jain teachings.

1st Edition
Production Team
Author: Allan Shepard
Editor: Luiz Santos
Cover: Studios Booklas / James Crawford
Consultant: Richard Evans
Researchers: Emily Watson, Thomas Blake, Sophia Grant
Typesetting: Mark Stevenson
Translation: Jonathan Carter
Publication and Identification
Ahimsa - The Timeless Wisdom of Jainism
Booklas, 2025
Categories: Religion / Philosophy / Spirituality
DDC: 181.44 - CDU: 294.4
All rights reserved to:
Luiz Antonio dos Santos ME / Booklas

No part of this book may be reproduced, stored in a retrieval system, or transmitted by any means—electronic, mechanical, photocopying, recording, or otherwise—without prior written permission from the copyright holder.

Summary

Prologue 11
Chapter 1 What is Jainism? 13
Chapter 2 Origins of Jainism 17
Chapter 3 The Last Tirthankara 22
Chapter 4 Jain Scriptures 27
Chapter 5 Core Principles of Jainism 32
Chapter 6 The Cornerstone of Jain Ethics 37
Chapter 7 The Jain Epistemology 42
Chapter 8 The Law of Spiritual Cause and Effect 48
Chapter 9 The Soul and the Non-Soul 54
Chapter 10 Bondage and Liberation 59
Chapter 11 Asceticism and Spiritual Practice 65
Chapter 12 The Path of Purification 71
Chapter 13 Jain Monasticism 79
Chapter 14 Jain Practices for Laymen and Laywomen 86
Chapter 15 The Jain Diet 93
Chapter 16 Jain Temples and Rituals 100
Chapter 17 Jain Art and Architecture 107
Chapter 18 Main Religious Festivals 114
Chapter 19 The Jain Community 122
Chapter 20 Jainism and Science 128
Chapter 21 Jainism and Environmentalism 134
Chapter 22 Peacebuilding 140
Chapter 23 Interreligious Dialogue 146

Chapter 24 Jainism in the Diaspora 152
Chapter 25 Contemporary Challenges 158
Chapter 26 The Future of Jainism.. 164
Chapter 27 Similarities with Buddhism..................................... 169
Chapter 28 The Enduring Legacy of Jainism............................ 174
Chapter 29 A Path to Inner Peace 180
Epilogue 184

Sistematic Index

Chapter 1: What is Jainism? - Introduces the reader to the concept of Jainism as a path to spiritual liberation through the purification of the soul, emphasizing non-violence (Ahimsa) above all else.

Chapter 2: Origins of Jainism - Explores the historical roots of Jainism in Ancient India, including its possible pre-Vedic origins and its relationship with other religions such as Hinduism and Buddhism.

Chapter 3: The Last Tirthankara - Delves into the life and teachings of Mahavira, the last Tirthankara of Jainism, highlighting his renunciation of worldly life, his attainment of enlightenment, and his role in revitalizing the Jain tradition.

Chapter 4: Jain Scriptures - Examines the Agamas, the sacred scriptures of Jainism, discussing their formation, divisions, languages, and importance in preserving and transmitting the teachings of the Tirthankaras.

Chapter 5: Core Principles of Jainism - Introduces the Three Jewels (Right View, Right Knowledge, Right Conduct) and the Five Great Vows (Ahimsa, Satya, Asteya, Brahmacharya, Aparigraha), the fundamental principles that guide Jain ethics and practice.

Chapter 6: The Cornerstone of Jain Ethics - Explores Ahimsa (Non-Violence) as the central ethical principle of Jainism, discussing its scope, philosophical basis, and practical implications in everyday life.

Chapter 7: The Jain Epistemology - Delves into Anekantavada and Syadvada, the Jain epistemological principles that emphasize the multiplicity of perspectives, the relativity of truth, and the importance of intellectual humility and tolerance.

Chapter 8: The Law of Spiritual Cause and Effect - Examines the Jain Theory of Karma, discussing the concept of Karma as a subtle substance, its different categories, the mechanisms of karmic bondage and liberation, and the importance of individual responsibility.

Chapter 9: The Soul and the Non-Soul - Explores the fundamental distinction between Jiva (Soul) and Ajiva (Non-Soul) in Jainism, discussing the nature of the soul, the categories of non-soul, and the interaction between them in conditioned experience.

Chapter 10: Bondage and Liberation - Discusses the concepts of Bandha (Bondage) and Moksha (Liberation), the ultimate goal of Jainism, exploring the state of karmic bondage, the path of liberation through the Three Jewels, and the characteristics of the liberated soul (Siddha).

Chapter 11: Asceticism and Spiritual Practice - Examines the role of asceticism (Tapas) in Jainism, discussing various ascetic practices such as fasting, meditation, self-discipline, and their importance in karmic purification and the pursuit of liberation.

Chapter 12: The Path of Purification - Explores the Fourteen Stages of Spiritual Development

(Gunasthanas) in Jainism, outlining the gradual progression of the soul towards liberation, and providing a map for self-understanding and spiritual progress.

Chapter 13: Jain Monasticism - Discusses the central role of monasticism in Jainism, exploring the two main monastic traditions, Digambara and Svetambara, and their differences and similarities in ascetic practice and the pursuit of liberation.

Chapter 14: Jain Practices for Laymen and Laywomen - Examines the Jain path for laypeople, discussing the Anuvratas (minor vows), additional ethical guidelines, and the importance of spiritual practice and social engagement for those living in the world.

Chapter 15: The Jain Diet - Explores the Jain diet and vegetarianism as expressions of Ahimsa, discussing the principles, practices, and benefits of Jain food choices for physical, mental, and spiritual health.

Chapter 16: Jain Temples and Rituals - Discusses the role of Jain temples (Derasar) and rituals in devotional practice, exploring their architecture, symbolism, ceremonies, and importance as centers of community and cultural preservation.

Chapter 17: Jain Art and Architecture - Explores the characteristics, symbolism, and aesthetics of Jain art and architecture, discussing the representations of Tirthankaras, the use of symbols, and the architectural elements of Jain temples.

Chapter 18: Main Religious Festivals - Discusses the main Jain festivals, such as Mahavir Jayanti, Paryushan Parva, Diwali, and Akshaya Tritiya, exploring their rituals, traditions, and spiritual significance.

Chapter 19: The Jain Community - Explores the structure and social engagement of the Jain community (Sangha), discussing its role in preserving the tradition, transmitting values, and contributing to society in areas such as education, health, and animal welfare.

Chapter 20: Jainism and Science - Discusses the relationship between Jainism and modern science, exploring parallels between Jain principles and scientific concepts, and identifying potential contributions of Jainism to an ethical and responsible science.

Chapter 21: Jainism and Environmentalism - Explores the ecological relevance of Jain Ahimsa, discussing the protection of all life forms, the rejection of the exploitation of nature, and the Jain ecological practices that promote sustainability and harmony with the environment.

Chapter 22: Peacebuilding - Discusses the Jain approach to peacebuilding, centered on Ahimsa as a tool for conflict resolution at all levels, emphasizing the importance of dialogue, mutual understanding, and empathy in building a more peaceful and harmonious world.

Chapter 23: Interreligious Dialogue - Explores the Jain perspective on religious diversity, based on Anekantavada and an ethic of respect and tolerance, discussing the Jain approach to interreligious dialogue and the search for universal values among different faith traditions.

Chapter 24: Jainism in the Diaspora - Discusses the expansion of Jainism outside India, the formation of Jain communities in the diaspora, and the challenges and adaptations faced in maintaining cultural and religious identity while contributing to the global dissemination of Jain teachings.

Chapter 25: Contemporary Challenges - Explores the internal and external challenges faced by Jainism in the modern world, discussing issues such as secularism, materialism, globalization, gender, social justice, and the modern adaptations and innovations in the practice and interpretation of Jainism.

Chapter 26: The Future of Jainism - Discusses the future prospects of Jainism, its potential to contribute to a more ethical, peaceful, and sustainable world, and the importance of preserving and promoting Jain teachings for future generations.

Chapter 27: Similarities with Buddhism - Presents a comparative analysis between Jainism and Buddhism, exploring their historical roots, ethical values, spiritual goals, and divergences in philosophical doctrines, ascetic practices, and approaches to liberation.

Chapter 28: The Enduring Legacy of Jainism - Explores the lasting impact of Jainism on Indian and global thought, discussing its influence on ethics, philosophy, vegetarianism, the animal rights movement, art, architecture, literature, and its core message of peace, non-violence, and spiritual seeking.

Chapter 29: A Path to Inner Peace - Concludes the book by recapping the central teachings and values of Jainism, emphasizing its potential as a path to inner peace and universal harmony, and reiterating its relevance in the contemporary world.

Prologue

Imagine an ancient path, trodden by sages who defied the illusions of the material world in search of ultimate truth. A path that traverses the centuries without bowing to the ephemeral changes of time, offering a code of conduct that transcends cultures and geographies. A path that not only teaches virtue, but embodies it, transforming every gesture, every word, every thought into an act of profound awareness and harmony with the universe.

This book you hold in your hands is not a simple historical account or a compendium of religious beliefs. It is an invitation to an inner journey, a gateway to understanding one of the most refined and radical philosophical systems ever conceived: Jainism.

From its origins in Ancient India to its silent, yet powerful, influence in the contemporary world, Jainism stands as a testament to the human soul's resistance to violence, ignorance, and attachment. Its doctrines are not merely abstract concepts; they are practical tools that can shape the way we perceive existence, interact with the world, and understand our role in the great tapestry of life.

The cornerstone of this tradition is Ahimsa – non-violence in its purest and most comprehensive expression. It is not just about avoiding physically harming another being, but about eliminating even the shadow of violence from our intentions and thoughts. What if true peace were not just a distant utopia, but a daily choice, cultivated with discipline and compassion?

Here, you will discover a universe where each soul is responsible for its own destiny, where truth is not rigid, but multifaceted, and where knowledge and right conduct are the only paths to liberation. This book does not merely present doctrines; it challenges you to see the world through a new lens, to question your habits, and to reflect on how each of your choices shapes not only your future, but the balance of all existence.

Do not expect an ordinary read. You are about to be guided through a labyrinth of profound ideas, to meet enlightened beings who transcended the limits of flesh and time, and to understand that truth is rarely absolute – it reveals itself in layers, like a gem that needs to be polished by experience and discernment.

This book is a gift, a map for those seeking a greater meaning in life. It does not impose dogmas, it does not demand blind faith – it merely illuminates a path that has always been before us, waiting to be recognized.

Welcome to this journey. Allow yourself to absorb each teaching, question each concept, feel each word resonate within you. For, at the end of this reading, you will not be the same.

The Editor.

Chapter 1
What is Jainism?

Jainism, one of the world's oldest religious and philosophical traditions, emanates from the vibrant and spiritually rich lands of Ancient India. Often mentioned alongside Buddhism, with which it shares roots and certain values, Jainism nevertheless possesses a distinct identity and a profound worldview that sets it apart. But what exactly is Jainism? At its core, it is a path, a philosophy of life, and a religious tradition that emphasizes non-violence (Ahimsa) above all else, seeking spiritual liberation (Moksha) through the purification of the soul.

To understand Jainism, it is crucial to detach oneself from Westernized conceptions of religion and spirituality. It is not merely a system of theological beliefs or dogmatic rituals, but rather a comprehensive set of ethical principles, ascetic practices, and a worldview that shapes all aspects of the lives of its practitioners. Imagine a philosophy that places individual responsibility at the center of the spiritual journey, where every action, every thought, every word has the power to influence the path towards liberation. That is the essence of Jainism.

The core values of Jainism revolve around the principle of Ahimsa, non-violence in all its forms – physical, verbal, and mental. It is not just about avoiding physically harming other beings, but about cultivating a deep compassion for all life, recognizing the soul (Jiva) present in every creature, no matter how small. This comprehensive vision of non-violence permeates all aspects of Jain ethics, from the strict vegetarian diet to the pursuit of professions that minimize any harm to other life forms.

Alongside Ahimsa, asceticism occupies a prominent place in Jainism. The fundamental belief is that attachment to the material world and sensory pleasures obscures the true nature of the soul and keeps it trapped in the cycle of birth, death, and rebirth. Therefore, ascetic practice, which involves self-discipline, fasting, meditation, and the reduction of material possessions, is seen as an essential means to purify the soul from Karma, the subtle substance that accumulates through actions and binds the soul to the material world.

Jainism is also distinguished by its unique epistemology, Anekantavada, the doctrine of the multiplicity of perspectives. This view recognizes that absolute truth is multifaceted and complex, and that no single perspective can grasp it completely. Instead of clinging to rigid dogmas, Jainism encourages intellectual humility and tolerance, encouraging the consideration of different points of view and avoiding hasty judgment. This epistemological approach is reflected in the logic of Syadvada, which uses conditional predication ("syat" – perhaps, in a certain sense) to express the complexity of reality and avoid absolute dogmatic assertions.

Originating in Ancient India, Jainism flourished in a rich and diverse cultural and religious context. Its emergence is often situated in the 6th century BCE, contemporary with the rise of Buddhism and other schools of thought that challenged the religious orthodoxies of the time. The central figure of modern Jainism is Mahavira, considered the last Tirthankara, a "Ford-Maker" or "Enlightened Teacher" who revitalized and systematized Jain teachings. However, the Jain tradition traces its origins much deeper into the past, believing in a succession of 24 Tirthankaras who are said to have manifested themselves throughout the ages to guide humanity on the path of liberation.

Although Jainism may be less well-known in the West than other Eastern religions, its relevance in the contemporary world is undeniable. In an era marked by conflict, violence, rampant consumerism, and environmental concerns, the Jain principles of non-violence, self-discipline, respect for all life, and the search for truth through multiple perspectives resonate with renewed urgency. The Jain message offers a path to inner peace, social harmony, and environmental sustainability, values increasingly essential for the survival and well-being of humanity and the planet.

Throughout this book, we will explore in detail the various facets of Jainism, from its historical origins and sacred scriptures to its philosophy, practices, lifestyle, and relevance in the modern world. We will delve into the principles of Ahimsa, Anekantavada, and Karma, unravel the ascetic and contemplative path, and examine the contributions of Jainism to ethics, ecology, and the pursuit of peace. Embark on this journey with us and discover the depth and beauty of Jainism: the path of non-violence that blossomed in India and continues to inspire millions of people around the world.

Chapter 2
Origins of Jainism

To unravel the history of Jainism, we are led to delve into the depths of time, into the remote eras of Ancient India, long before the historical records we know. The origins of Jainism are lost in the mists of prehistory, with theories pointing to pre-Vedic roots, suggesting that this tradition may be even older than Hinduism itself and the Vedic system that gave rise to it. This fascinating perspective invites us to rethink the traditional chronology of Indian religions and to consider the possibility of a continuous spiritual flow that precedes the categorizations we impose today.

One of the most intriguing theories about the origins of Jainism lies in the hypothesis of an autochthonous ascetic tradition of India, which flourished before the arrival of the Indo-Aryan peoples and Vedic culture. Archaeological evidence, such as seals and artifacts from the Indus Valley Civilization (Harappa and Mohenjo-daro), reveals figures in meditative postures and representations of revered animals, which some scholars interpret as precursors of Jain concepts and practices. These findings fuel the speculation that a current of ascetic and non-violent thought already existed in India before the formation of

Vedic Hinduism, and that Jainism could be the heir to this ancestral tradition.

When contrasting Jainism with the other currents of thought in Ancient India, such as Buddhism and Hinduism, we perceive both parallels and significant divergences. It is undeniable that Jainism and Buddhism share common ground, emerging in the same historical and geographical period, and both challenging the caste system and the authority of Vedic rituals. Both traditions emphasize the importance of non-violence, ethics, and the pursuit of liberation from the cycle of suffering. However, their approaches and doctrines diverge on crucial points.

While Buddhism, in its early development, focused on the Middle Way and a more pragmatic approach to spiritual practice, Jainism has always been characterized by radical asceticism and an emphasis on the extreme purification of the soul. The Jain doctrine of the Soul (Jiva) as an individual, eternal, and inherently pure entity, which is imprisoned by matter and Karma, contrasts with the Buddhist doctrine of Non-Self (Anatta), which denies the existence of a substantial and permanent soul. This fundamental difference in the view of the soul profoundly influences the practices and spiritual goals of each tradition.

In relation to Hinduism, the relationship is even more complex. Although Jainism developed in a cultural context that also gave rise to Hinduism, it represents, in many aspects, a critique and a deviation from Vedic practices and beliefs. Jainism rejects the authority of the Vedas, the caste system, ritual sacrifices, and the polytheistic theology of Vedic Hinduism. Instead, it proposes a path of self-liberation through asceticism and non-violence, focused on the individual purification of the soul and the pursuit of enlightenment. However, throughout history, Jainism and Hinduism have coexisted and interacted, influencing each other in areas such as ethics, philosophy, and devotional practices.

A central concept for understanding the origins and evolution of Jainism is the figure of the Tirthankaras. In Jainism, it is believed that the Dharma (the teaching and the path of righteousness) is revealed in each era by exceptional enlightened beings, the Tirthankaras, which literally means "Ford-makers" or "Those who Cross the River". They are seen as supreme examples of spiritual perfection, having achieved liberation (Moksha) and shown the way for others to follow. The Jain tradition recognizes 24 Tirthankaras in each cosmic cycle of time, with Rishabhanatha being the first and Mahavira the last Tirthankara of this era.

The importance of the Tirthankaras lies in the fact that they are not considered gods or divine avatars, but rather human beings who, through their own effort and ascetic practice, have achieved enlightenment and become spiritual guides for humanity. Their lives and teachings serve as models for Jain practitioners, inspiring them to follow the path of non-violence, asceticism, and the pursuit of liberation. The belief in a continuous succession of Tirthankaras over time also reinforces the idea that the Jain Dharma is eternal and universal, always available to those who seek the truth.

The archaeological and literary evidence of the early Jain communities provides us with valuable clues about the early history of this tradition. Inscriptions on rocks, pillars, and stupas, dating from the 3rd and 2nd centuries BC, mention Jain monks and nuns, indicating the existence of an organized monastic community already in a very ancient period. Early Jain art, found in archaeological sites such as Mathura and Sanchi, reveals representations of the Tirthankaras and scenes of monastic life, confirming the presence and influence of Jainism in different regions of India.

In the field of literature, the Agamas, the sacred Jain scriptures, although compiled in their written form later, preserve oral traditions and teachings that date back to the time of Mahavira and possibly to even earlier periods. These canonical texts offer a glimpse into the doctrine, ethics, practices, and organization of the early Jain community. References to Jainism can also be found in other literary sources of Ancient India, such as Buddhist and Hindu texts, which, although often presenting external and sometimes critical perspectives, corroborate the antiquity and relevance of Jainism in the religious landscape of the time.

In summary, the historical origins of Jainism remain shrouded in mystery and debate, but the available evidence points to a rich and complex tradition, with deep roots in Ancient India. Whether as the heir to a pre-Vedic tradition, as a reform movement within the Vedic context, or as an original current of thought that emerged in the 6th century BC, Jainism established itself as a lasting spiritual and philosophical force, shaping Indian culture and offering a unique path to spiritual liberation. In the following chapters, we will continue to explore the fascinating journey of Jainism, delving into the life of Mahavira, the sacred scriptures, and the fundamental principles that define this ancient and relevant tradition.

Chapter 3
The Last Tirthankara

In the vast panorama of Jain history, the figure of Mahavira emerges with a singular brilliance, as the last Tirthankara of this era, the 24th in the lineage. While the previous Tirthankaras are lost in the mists of mythical time, Mahavira's life is more firmly anchored in a historical context, allowing us to trace a more detailed biographical profile and understand the transformative impact of his existence and teachings. Born as a prince, Mahavira renounced wealth and power to embrace a radical ascetic path, achieving enlightenment and revitalizing the Jain Dharma for ages to come.

The historical and social context of Mahavira's birth is crucial to understanding the uniqueness of his journey. He was born in the 6th century BC, in a time of intellectual and religious effervescence in Ancient India. This was the period when new currents of thought challenged the Vedic traditions, questioning the caste system, sacrificial rituals, and the pursuit of material rewards. Buddhism was also flourishing at this time, and other ascetic and philosophical sects were emerging, seeking alternative paths to spiritual liberation. In this scenario of transformation and questioning, Jainism, under the leadership of Mahavira, found fertile ground to develop and disseminate its teachings.

Jain tradition reports that Mahavira was born in Kundagrama, near Vaishali, in the region of Bihar, India, into a Kshatriya family (warrior caste). His birth name was Vardhamana, which means "the one who increases" or "the prosperous," reflecting the expectations of greatness that surrounded his birth. His father, Siddhartha, was the head of a clan called Jnatrika, and his mother, Trishala, was the sister of King Chetaka of Vaishali. Therefore, Mahavira was born into an environment of nobility and privilege, destined for a life of power and material comfort.

However, from an early age, Vardhamana demonstrated an inclination towards introspection and renunciation. Unlike other young nobles, he was not attracted to the pleasures of palace life, games, hunting, or the pursuit of political power. Instead, he sought solitude, meditation, and contemplation, questioning the meaning of life and the suffering inherent in human existence. This deep spiritual unrest prevented him from being content with worldly life and propelled him towards a deeper search.

At the age of thirty, after the death of his parents, Vardhamana made the radical decision to renounce the material world. In an act of courage and detachment, he abandoned his life as a prince, his family, his wealth, and all material comforts to become an ascetic monk. This renunciation was not an impulsive act, but rather the result of deep reflection and a sincere desire to find truth and liberation. Jain tradition describes this event as

Diksha, the monastic initiation, a crucial moment in Mahavira's life and in the development of Jainism.

The period of asceticism and intense spiritual search that followed the renunciation was marked by twelve years of rigorous self-discipline, deep meditation, and extreme austerity. Mahavira wandered as a wandering ascetic, devoid of material possessions, clothes, or a fixed shelter. He practiced prolonged fasting, often abstaining from food and water for days or weeks at a time. He endured the elements, the scorching heat of the Indian summer and the biting cold of winter, without seeking refuge or protection. He faced the hostility of ignorant people and insect bites, without retaliating or getting angry.

During this period of extreme asceticism, Mahavira practiced Ahimsa in its most radical form. He avoided harming any form of life, however small, in thought, word, or deed. He walked carefully to avoid stepping on insects, used a cloth over his mouth to avoid swallowing airborne microorganisms, and swept the ground in front of him to avoid harming any creature. This meticulous practice of non-violence became a hallmark of Jain asceticism and an inspiring example for his followers.

After twelve years of intense ascetic practice and deep meditation, Mahavira attained supreme enlightenment, Kevala Jnana, perfect and infinite knowledge. This transcendental moment marked the end of his spiritual quest and the beginning of his mission as a Tirthankara, an enlightened guide for humanity. Jain tradition describes Mahavira's enlightenment as a cosmic event, accompanied by signs and wonders, indicating the importance and uniqueness of his achievement.

After enlightenment (Kevala Jnana), Mahavira began his preaching, dedicating the rest of his life to sharing his teachings and showing the path of liberation to others. He traveled to various regions of India, teaching in simple and accessible language, attracting followers from all social classes, including kings, nobles, merchants, artisans, and humble people. His central message was the path of Ahimsa, self-discipline, and purification of the soul as means to achieve liberation from suffering and the cycle of reincarnation.

To disseminate his teachings effectively, Mahavira organized the sangha, the Jain monastic community, composed of monks (Sadhu) and nuns (Sadhvi). He established rules and guidelines for monastic life, emphasizing Ahimsa, truth, non-covetousness, chastity, and detachment. The sangha became the core of the Jain tradition, preserving and transmitting Mahavira's teachings throughout the centuries. In addition to the monastic community, Mahavira also attracted a large number of laymen and laywomen (Shravaka and Shravika), who followed Jain principles in their daily lives, practicing the Anuvratas, the lesser vows adapted to lay life.

Mahavira's legacy is immense and enduring. He is revered as the last Tirthankara, the spiritual guide who revitalized and systematized Jainism for the present era. His teachings on Ahimsa, self-discipline, non-possessiveness, Anekantavada, and the pursuit of liberation continue to inspire millions of people around the world. The Jain sangha, founded by Mahavira, has flourished over the centuries, preserving the tradition and disseminating its values. Jainism, as we know it today, is largely the result of the life, teachings, and transformative legacy of Mahavira, the last Tirthankara, the spiritual lion who roared the message of non-violence and liberation to all humanity.

Chapter 4
Jain Scriptures

Beyond the exemplary life of Mahavira, the Jain tradition bequeathed to the world a vast and complex body of sacred scriptures, known as the Agamas. These scriptures, which literally translate to "that which has come down from tradition" or "that which has been transmitted," represent the very backbone of Jainism, the primary source of its teachings, doctrines, practices, and history. The Agamas are not merely religious texts in the conventional sense, but rather the codified expression of the Jain Dharma, the path of righteousness and liberation revealed by the Tirthankaras and preserved over the generations.

The fundamental concept behind the Agamas is Shruta Jnana, "heard knowledge" or "orally transmitted knowledge." In the Jain tradition, it is believed that the teachings of the Tirthankaras were originally transmitted orally by their direct disciples, the Gandharas and the Shrutakevalins. These enlightened beings possessed the ability to memorize and faithfully transmit the words of the Tirthankaras, ensuring the purity and authenticity of the tradition. For centuries, Shruta Jnana was preserved orally, recited, memorized, and transmitted from master to disciple, forming the basis of the Jain tradition.

The formation of the Jain canon, that is, the compilation of the Agamas in written form, is a complex and multifaceted process, which spanned several centuries. Although the oral tradition was paramount in the early centuries of Jainism, the need to preserve the teachings in the face of the vicissitudes of time and potential memory loss led to the gradual writing of the Agamas. The canonization process was not linear or unified, and different Jain sects, such as the Digambaras and the Svetambaras, eventually developed distinct scriptural canons, reflecting the particularities of their traditions and interpretations.

For the Svetambaras, the "white-clad" Jain sect, the complete Agama canon consists of 45 texts, divided into several categories. The main divisions of the Svetambara Agamas are the Angas, the Upangas, the Prakirnakas, the Chedasutras, the Mulasutras, and the Anuyogadvaras. The Angas (limbs) are considered the oldest and most important texts, containing the essential teachings of Mahavira. The Upangas (secondary limbs) expand and complement the teachings of the Angas. The Prakirnakas (miscellaneous texts) address a variety of doctrinal and practical topics. The Chedasutras (disciplinary texts) deal with the rules and regulations for monastic life. The Mulasutras (root texts) provide the foundations of Jain doctrine and practice. And the Anuyogadvaras (gateways to exposition) offer methods for the interpretation and study of the Agamas.

The Digambaras, the "sky-clad" Jain sect, have a different view of the Agama canon. They believe that the original Agamas, the Purvas (ancient texts), were lost long ago, and that the texts currently available, known as Angabahyas (external to the Angas), are of secondary authority. However, the Digambaras also revere a set of important scriptures, such as the Shatkhandagama, the Kashayapahuda, the Samayasara, the Pravachanasara, and the Niyamasara, which they consider to preserve the essence of the Jain teachings. The divergence in scriptural canons between Svetambaras and Digambaras reflects the historical and doctrinal differences that arose over time between the two sects.

The sacred languages of the Agamas are primarily Ardhamagadhi and Sanskrit. Ardhamagadhi, an ancient form of Prakrit, was the vernacular language spoken in the region of Magadha, where Mahavira preached and where Jainism initially flourished. It is believed that Mahavira taught in Ardhamagadhi to reach the common people and make his teachings accessible to all. Later, Sanskrit, the classical language of India, was also used in the composition and interpretation of the Agamas, especially in commentaries and philosophical works. The use of both languages reflects the cultural and linguistic diversity of the context in which Jainism developed.

The interpretation and importance of the scriptures in Jain practice are complex and multifaceted topics. The Agamas are not seen as dogmatic or inflexible texts, but rather as guides for spiritual practice and understanding of the Dharma. The Jain tradition recognizes the need for interpretation (Niryukti) to understand the deeper meaning of the Agamas, taking into account the historical, cultural, and doctrinal context. Extensive commentaries have been written over the centuries by Jain scholars, seeking to elucidate the teachings of the Agamas and make them relevant to different times and contexts.

The importance of the scriptures in Jain life is multifaceted. The Agamas serve as a source of doctrinal authority, defining the fundamental principles of Jainism, such as Ahimsa, Karma, Moksha, and Anekantavada. They provide ethical guidance for moral conduct, both for monks and nuns and for laymen and laywomen. They offer spiritual practices such as meditation, asceticism, study, and devotion, as means for the purification of the soul and the pursuit of liberation. They also narrate the history of the Tirthankaras and the Jain community, transmitting the cultural and religious heritage of the tradition.

The study of the Agamas (Agama Adhyayana) is considered a meritorious spiritual practice in itself. Jains are encouraged to read, listen to, recite, memorize, and contemplate the scriptures, seeking to deepen their understanding of the Dharma and strengthen their faith. The study of the Agamas is not just an intellectual exercise, but a form of immersion in the wisdom of the Tirthankaras, a means of connecting with the tradition and receiving inspiration and guidance for the spiritual journey. The Agamas are seen as an invaluable treasure, a beacon that illuminates the path to liberation and offers a safe guide for those who seek truth and inner peace.

In summary, the Jain scriptures, the Agamas, represent a precious legacy of the tradition, the voice of the Tirthankaras echoing through the centuries. Their complex formation, their diverse divisions, their sacred languages, and their rich history of interpretation reflect the depth and vitality of Jainism. The Agamas are not just ancient texts, but living sources of wisdom and guidance, which continue to inspire and guide Jain practitioners on the path of non-violence, self-discipline, and the pursuit of spiritual liberation. In the next chapter, we will explore the core principles of Jainism, the Three Jewels and the Five Great Vows, which derive directly from the teachings of the Agamas and form the basis of Jain ethics and practice.

Chapter 5
Core Principles of Jainism

At the beating heart of the Jain tradition lies a set of core principles that act as a compass and guide on the spiritual journey towards liberation. These principles, elegantly synthesized in the Three Jewels (Ratnatraya) and the Five Great Vows (Mahavratas), offer a clear map and a practical path for the purification of the soul, overcoming suffering, and achieving inner peace. They are not mere dogmas or arbitrary rules, but rather the fundamental pillars of Jain ethics and practice, interconnected and interdependent, forming a coherent and comprehensive system for spiritual transformation.

The Three Jewels (Ratnatraya), also known as the "Three Paths of Liberation," represent the essential foundations for the Jain spiritual journey. They are: Right View (Samyak Darshana), Right Knowledge (Samyak Jnana), and Right Conduct (Samyak Charitra). These three jewels are not separate entities, but rather interdependent facets of the same path, complementing and reinforcing each other. Just as a multifaceted jewel shines in different directions, the Three Jewels illuminate the Jain spiritual path from different perspectives, leading the practitioner to true realization.

Right View (Samyak Darshana) is the starting point, the foundation upon which the other jewels rest. It refers to rational faith and conviction in the fundamental principles of Jainism, such as the existence of the soul (Jiva), the law of Karma, the possibility of liberation (Moksha), and the validity of the Jain path to achieve it. It is not a blind or dogmatic faith, but rather an intellectual and intuitive understanding of the Jain truth, based on study, reflection, and experience. Right View implies seeing the world and oneself according to the Jain perspective, recognizing the reality of the soul, Karma, and the cycle of reincarnation, and aspiring to liberation as the ultimate goal of life.

Right Knowledge (Samyak Jnana) is the second jewel, which develops from Right View. It refers to the correct and precise understanding of Jain doctrine, obtained through the study of scriptures (Agamas), learning from spiritual teachers, and contemplation. Right Knowledge is not merely the accumulation of intellectual information, but rather the deep and experiential understanding of Jain principles, which translates into wisdom and discernment. It includes knowledge about the nature of the soul, Karma, the stages of the spiritual journey (Gunasthanas), ascetic practices, and the path to liberation. Right Knowledge enables the practitioner to discern right from wrong, to make ethical decisions, and to tread the spiritual path with clarity and purpose.

Right Conduct (Samyak Charitra) is the third jewel, the culmination of the previous two. It refers to ethical and moral practice in accordance with Jain principles, especially Ahimsa (non-violence). Right Conduct encompasses all aspects of life, from physical and verbal actions to thoughts and intentions. It implies living according to Jain vows, practicing asceticism, meditation, self-discipline, and cultivating virtues such as compassion, honesty, non-covetousness, and detachment. Right Conduct is the practical side of the spiritual journey, the concrete application of Jain principles in everyday life, aiming at the purification of Karma and progress towards liberation.

The Three Jewels are concretely manifested in the Five Great Vows (Mahavratas), which represent the fundamental ethical precepts for Jain monks and nuns, those who have completely renounced worldly life and dedicated themselves entirely to the spiritual path. These five vows are: Ahimsa (Non-Violence), Satya (Truth), Asteya (Non-Stealing), Brahmacharya (Chastity), and Aparigraha (Non-Possessiveness). They represent the ultimate expression of Jain ethics and a rigorous guide for moral and spiritual conduct.

Ahimsa (Non-Violence), as already mentioned, is the cornerstone of Jain ethics. The First Great Vow requires absolute non-violence in thought, word, and deed, towards all living beings, from the largest animals to the smallest microorganisms. For monks and nuns, this means an extreme commitment to non-violence, avoiding any form of harm or suffering to any creature. They follow strict rules in their diet, their movements, and their interactions with the world, seeking to minimize any negative impact on other life forms.

Satya (Truth), the Second Great Vow, requires absolute truthfulness in all situations. It means abstaining from lying, deceiving, distorting the truth, or using language in a harmful way. For Jain ascetics, the pursuit of truth is fundamental, and the word must be used with care and responsibility, always seeking clarity, honesty, and non-violence in communication.

Asteya (Non-Stealing), the Third Great Vow, requires complete abstention from stealing or taking anything that has not been freely given. For monks and nuns, this means not only avoiding theft in the conventional sense, but also not accepting anything that is not offered spontaneously, living with simplicity and contentment with what is essential for survival.

Brahmacharya (Chastity), the Fourth Great Vow, requires total abstinence from sexual activity and the practice of absolute celibacy. For Jain ascetics, sexual energy is seen as a powerful force that can divert the mind from the spiritual quest and create attachment to the material world. Brahmacharya aims to channel this energy into spiritual practice, promoting mental purity and self-discipline.

Aparigraha (Non-Possessiveness), the Fifth Great Vow, requires complete detachment from material goods and the reduction of possessions to the bare minimum. For monks and nuns, this means living without possessions, depending on the charity of lay people for basic needs such as food, clothing, and shelter. Aparigraha aims to overcome attachment to the material world, recognizing that true wealth lies in the soul and not in external possessions.

For laymen and laywomen (Shravakas and Shravikas), who live in the world and have not renounced family and professional life, the Five Lesser Vows (Anuvratas) are prescribed. These vows represent an adaptation of the Five Great Vows for lay life, allowing Jain practitioners to follow ethical principles in their daily context, without the extreme rigor of monasticism. The Anuvratas are Ahimsa Anuvrata (Lesser Non-Violence), Satya Anuvrata (Lesser Truth), Asteya Anuvrata (Lesser Non-Stealing), Brahmacharya Anuvrata (Lesser Chastity), and Aparigraha Anuvrata (Lesser Non-Possessiveness). Although less rigorous than the Mahavratas, the Anuvratas represent a serious commitment to Jain ethics and a gradual path to purification and spiritual progress in lay life.

In short, the Three Jewels and the Five Great Vows (and Anuvratas) constitute the core of Jain ethics and practice. They represent an interconnected system of principles that aim at the complete transformation of the individual, from worldview and intellectual knowledge to moral conduct and spiritual practices. By following this path, Jains seek to purify their souls of Karma, overcome suffering, and achieve final liberation (Moksha), the state of infinite peace, bliss, and knowledge. In the following chapters, we will explore each of these principles in depth, unveiling their nuances and implications for Jain life and for the contemporary world.

Chapter 6
The Cornerstone of Jain Ethics

If there is one principle that defines and permeates Jainism in its entirety, that principle is, undoubtedly, Ahimsa, non-violence. More than a mere ethical precept, Ahimsa ascends to the status of a cornerstone, the foundation upon which the entire moral, spiritual, and practical structure of Jainism is built. It is not just a recommendation to avoid violence, but rather an absolute imperative, an unwavering commitment to non-aggression and respect for each and every form of life, in all dimensions of existence. Understanding the depth and breadth of Ahimsa is essential to entering the Jain universe and glimpsing its unique contribution to world ethics and spirituality.

The definition and scope of the concept of Ahimsa in Jainism far surpasses the superficial understanding of physical non-violence. Ahimsa is not limited to avoiding acts of physical aggression against other human beings or animals. It crucially encompasses verbal and mental non-violence. In fact, Jainism emphasizes that violence can manifest itself on three distinct levels: through the body (physical), speech (verbal), and thought (mental). Each of these levels is equally important and interconnected, and the true practitioner of Ahimsa seeks to cultivate non-violence in all three dimensions.

Physical non-violence (Kayik Ahimsa) refers to abstaining from any act that causes physical harm, suffering, or death to any living being. This includes not only direct acts of violence, such as physical assault or murder, but also indirect actions that may result in harm, such as the exploitation of animals, the destruction of the environment, or neglect of the well-being of other creatures. The strict Jain vegetarianism, for example, is a direct expression of Kayik Ahimsa, seeking to avoid any participation in the violence inherent in the production of meat and other animal products.

Verbal non-violence (Vachik Ahimsa) concerns the use of language in a peaceful, honest, and constructive way. It implies avoiding words that may hurt, insult, defame, deceive, or cause emotional suffering to others. Vachik Ahimsa encourages compassionate, kind, and truthful communication, always seeking harmony, mutual understanding, and peaceful conflict resolution. Silence, in certain situations, can be considered a form of Vachik Ahimsa, when speaking could generate discord or violence.

Mental non-violence (Manasik Ahimsa), perhaps the most subtle and challenging dimension of Ahimsa, refers to the purification of the mind from violent, aggressive, hateful, or harmful thoughts. It implies cultivating benevolence, compassion, empathy, and love in relation to all beings. Manasik Ahimsa seeks to eradicate the roots of violence in the mind itself, recognizing that thoughts are the precursors of words and actions. Meditation and mental self-discipline are essential practices for cultivating Manasik Ahimsa and transforming the mind into an instrument of peace and harmony.

The philosophical basis of Ahimsa in Jainism lies in the concept of Jiva. Jiva, in Jainism, refers to the individual soul, the pure and eternal consciousness that animates all living beings. The fundamental belief is that all living beings, from humans to the smallest microorganisms, possess Jiva and, therefore, possess the same capacity to feel pain, suffering, and joy. This vision of unity and interconnectedness of all life underlies the Jain respect for all forms of life and the imperative of Ahimsa.

Ahimsa as respect for all forms of life (Jiva) means recognizing the sacredness and dignity inherent in every living creature. It is not about hierarchizing life forms or considering some more valuable than others. For the Jain, all life is precious and deserves to be protected and respected. This comprehensive view of life extends not only to animals, but also to plants, insects, microorganisms, and even the elements of nature, such as water and air, which are considered to possess subtle forms of Jiva. This profound reverence for life is what motivates radical vegetarianism, ascetic practices, and the Jain lifestyle.

The practical implications of Ahimsa in daily life are vast and comprehensive. They permeate all aspects of Jain existence, from food and profession to behavior and social relations. In food, Ahimsa manifests itself in strict vegetarianism, which excludes meat, fish, eggs, and, in some Jain traditions, even roots and tubers, as they are considered to involve the death or suffering of living beings. The Jain diet is based on grains, legumes, fruits, vegetables, and dairy products (for those who do not follow vegan vegetarianism), seeking to minimize the impact on other life forms as much as possible.

In profession, Jains are encouraged to choose activities that are compatible with the principle of Ahimsa, avoiding professions that involve violence, exploitation of animals, or damage to the environment. Professions such as medicine, teaching, social service, the arts, and fair trade are seen as more aligned with Jain values than professions such as hunting, fishing, slaughtering animals, weapons production, or activities that cause pollution and environmental destruction.

In everyday behavior, Ahimsa is expressed in kindness, compassion, honesty, tolerance, and respect for all beings. Jains are encouraged to avoid anger, hatred, jealousy, pride, and other negative emotions that can lead to violence. They seek to cultivate patience, humility, generosity, and empathy, always seeking the well-being and happiness of all.

Ahimsa and universal compassion (Karuna) are intrinsically linked concepts in Jainism. Ahimsa is not only the absence of violence, but also the active presence of compassion and love for all beings. Karuna, universal compassion, is the emotion that arises naturally from the understanding of the interconnectedness of all life and the recognition of the suffering of others as our own suffering. Jain compassion is not limited to human beings, but extends to all living beings, without distinction. It motivates altruistic action, selfless service, and the pursuit of alleviating suffering in all its forms.

Finally, Ahimsa as a path to inner and outer peace reveals its profound relevance both on the individual and collective levels. By cultivating non-violence in all dimensions of life, the Jain practitioner seeks to achieve inner peace, mental serenity, and liberation from the cycle of suffering. Ahimsa purifies the mind of negative emotions, calms the passions, and promotes inner harmony. At the same time, Ahimsa contributes to external peace, the construction of a more just, peaceful, and sustainable society. The Jain message of non-violence resonates with urgency in a world marked by conflict, war, and inequality, offering a path for personal and social transformation, towards a future of peace and universal harmony.

In summary, Jain Ahimsa is much more than the simple absence of violence. It is a comprehensive and profound ethical principle, a complete spiritual path that permeates all aspects of life. By embracing Ahimsa in its entirety, the Jain seeks to purify his soul, cultivate universal compassion, and contribute to inner and outer peace. Ahimsa, the cornerstone of Jain ethics, is a beacon of hope in a troubled world, an invitation to personal and social transformation, and a path to the realization of true human nature: the nature of peace, love, and non-violence.

Chapter 7
The Jain Epistemology

In the intricate philosophical edifice of Jainism, two epistemological pillars stand out, giving uniqueness and depth to its worldview: Anekantavada and Syadvada. These concepts, intrinsically linked and complementary, represent the Jain approach to understanding reality, knowledge, and truth. Far from dogmatism and absolute assertions, Jainism, through Anekantavada and Syadvada, proposes a relativistic, open, and tolerant epistemology, recognizing the inherent complexity of existence and the limitation of the human perspective to grasp it in its entirety. To explore these concepts is to delve into the heart of Jain philosophy and unveil its unique view on the nature of knowledge and truth.

Anekantavada, which translates as "non-one-sidedness doctrine" or "doctrine of the multiplicity of aspects," is the Jain principle of metaphysical and epistemological relativism. At its core, Anekantavada asserts that reality is multifaceted, complex, and has numerous aspects. No object, event, or concept can be fully understood from a single perspective, as truth is relative to the point of view, time, place, and circumstances. This doctrine challenges the linear and dualistic view of reality, proposing a richer and more nuanced understanding that recognizes the diversity and interconnectedness of all phenomena.

The fundamental implication of Anekantavada is the relativity of truth. For Jainism, there is no absolute, single, and immutable truth accessible to a single perspective. Truth is always partial, relative, and dependent on the observer's point of view. Each perspective reveals only one aspect of reality, and the complete understanding of truth requires the integration of multiple perspectives, the consideration of different angles, and the overcoming of a one-sided view. This relativity of truth does not imply skepticism or nihilism, but rather epistemological humility and intellectual tolerance.

Syadvada, the "doctrine of 'Syat'" or "doctrine of conditional predication," is the logical and linguistic expression of Anekantavada. Syat, in Sanskrit, means "perhaps," "possibly," "in a certain sense." Syadvada proposes that all statements about reality should be qualified with the adverb "Syat," indicating that they are only partially true, valid only under certain conditions and perspectives. This logic of conditional predication aims to avoid dogmatic and absolute statements, recognizing the limitation of language and the human mind to express the complexity of reality.

Syadvada manifests itself in the form of Saptabhangi, the "logic of seven predications" or "seven modes of predication." Saptabhangi is a logical system that uses seven propositions to express the complexity of any statement about reality, considering different perspectives and possibilities. The seven propositions are:

Syat asti: "In a certain sense, it is" (Affirmation of existence from one perspective).

Syat nasti: "In a certain sense, it is not" (Negation of existence from another perspective).

Syat asti ca nasti ca: "In a certain sense, it is and it is not" (Simultaneous affirmation and negation from different perspectives).

Syat avaktavyam: "In a certain sense, it is indescribable" (Total inexpressibility from one perspective).

Syat asti ca avaktavyam ca: "In a certain sense, it is and it is indescribable" (Simultaneous affirmation and inexpressibility from different perspectives).

Syat nasti ca avaktavyam ca: "In a certain sense, it is not and it is indescribable" (Simultaneous negation and inexpressibility from different perspectives).

Syat asti ca nasti ca avaktavyam ca: "In a certain sense, it is, it is not, and it is indescribable" (Simultaneous affirmation, negation, and inexpressibility from different perspectives).

Saptabhangi should not be interpreted as a form of confusion or indecision, but rather as a tool for the deep and multifaceted analysis of reality. By using the conditional logic of Syadvada, Jainism seeks to avoid dogmatism, rigidity, and a one-sided view, promoting mental flexibility, openness to different perspectives, and the understanding of the complexity inherent in truth.

To assist in the application of Anekantavada and Syadvada, Jainism uses Nayavada, the "doctrine of viewpoints" or "doctrine of partial perspectives." Naya means "point of view," "perspective," "angle of vision." Nayavada recognizes that there are numerous possible viewpoints to approach any reality, each revealing a particular and partial aspect of the truth. By using Nayavada, Jainism invites us to consider different perspectives before forming a judgment or reaching a conclusion, recognizing that no single perspective is sufficient to grasp the totality of truth.

Nayavada classifies viewpoints into various categories, such as Dravyarthikanaya (substantial viewpoint), which focuses on the substance or permanent essence of an object, and Paryayarthikanaya (modal viewpoint), which focuses on the changing qualities and modes of an object. By considering both viewpoints, for example, we can understand that a soul (Jiva) is substantially eternal and immutable (Dravyarthikanaya), but also manifests through different states and changing qualities (Paryayarthikanaya) throughout the cycle of reincarnation. Nayavada helps us avoid a reductionist and one-sided view, integrating different perspectives for a more complete and balanced understanding.

The importance of intellectual humility and tolerance in Jain philosophy derives directly from Anekantavada and Syadvada. By recognizing the relativity of truth and the limitation of the human perspective, Jainism promotes an attitude of intellectual humility, which acknowledges that our knowledge is always partial and incomplete, and that we are always subject to errors and mistakes. This intellectual humility leads us to tolerance, respect for different opinions and beliefs, and openness to dialogue and learning from others. Jainism teaches us to avoid hasty judgment, condemning the opinions of others, and dogmatically clinging to our own beliefs, recognizing that truth can manifest itself in various forms and from different perspectives.

Finally, Anekantavada and Syadvada, as tools for resolving conflicts and promoting dialogue, reveal their profound practical and social relevance. In a world marked by ideological, religious, and political conflicts, Jain epistemology offers a path to mutual understanding, the peaceful resolution of disagreements, and the building of bridges between different perspectives. By recognizing that each side of a conflict may have a portion of the truth, that different opinions may be valid from different points of view, and that complete truth emerges from dialogue and the integration of multiple perspectives, Anekantavada and Syadvada empower us to overcome dogmatism, intolerance, and a one-sided view, promoting social harmony, cooperation, and the search for consensual solutions.

In summary, Anekantavada and Syadvada, the Jain epistemology, represent a unique contribution to world philosophy and spirituality. By proposing a relativistic view of truth, conditional logic, and the use of multiple perspectives, Jainism invites us to overcome dogmatism, intolerance, and a one-sided view, cultivating intellectual humility, tolerance, dialogue, and the search for a richer and more complete understanding of reality. These epistemological principles are not just philosophical abstractions, but practical tools for everyday life, empowering us to build more harmonious relationships, resolve conflicts peacefully, and walk the spiritual path with wisdom, discernment, and open-mindedness. In the next chapter, we will explore the Theory of Karma in Jainism, unveiling the law of spiritual cause and effect that underlies Jain ethics and practice, and which is deeply connected to the relativistic epistemology of Anekantavada and Syadvada.

Chapter 8
The Law of Spiritual Cause and Effect

In the intricate philosophical system of Jainism, the Theory of Karma occupies a central place, acting as the mainspring that drives the wheel of existence, shaping the experiences of every living being and propelling the spiritual journey towards liberation. Unlike other conceptions of Karma present in other Indian traditions, Jainism offers a unique and deeply detailed view of Karma, not as a predetermined destiny or an abstract force, but rather as a subtle, material and real substance that accumulates in the soul (Jiva) in response to the actions, thoughts and intentions of each individual. Unraveling the Jain Theory of Karma is crucial to understanding the ethics, ascetic practice and the ultimate goal of liberation (Moksha) within this tradition.

The concept of Karma as a subtle substance is one of the distinctive features of Jain theory. In Jainism, Karma is not merely a moral law of cause and effect, but rather an almost physical entity, subtle Pudgala (matter), which adheres to the soul, obscuring its inherent purity and imprisoning it in the cycle of birth, death and rebirth. This karmic substance is described as being extremely fine and subtle, penetrating the soul and influencing its cognitive, emotional and volitional faculties. The metaphor often used is that of fine dust that accumulates on a mirror, obscuring its ability to reflect light. Likewise, Karma obscures the pure and luminous nature of the soul, preventing it from manifesting its maximum potential.

There are different categories of Karma in Jainism, classified based on their effects and how they influence the soul. The main distinction is between Ghatiya Karma (Obstructive Karmas) and Aghatiya Karma (Non-Obstructive Karmas). Ghatiya Karmas are those that obstruct the intrinsic faculties of the soul, preventing it from manifesting its infinite knowledge, infinite perception, infinite bliss and infinite power. There are four main types of Ghatiya Karma:

Jnanavaraniya Karma (Karma that obscures knowledge): Prevents the soul from achieving Right Knowledge (Samyak Jnana), generating ignorance and delusion.

Darshanavaraniya Karma (Karma that obscures perception): Prevents the soul from achieving Right View (Samyak Darshana), generating disbelief and a distorted view of reality.

Mohaniya Karma (Karma that generates illusion): Obscures the soul's ability to experience true bliss, generating attachment, aversion, passions and disturbing emotions.

Antaraya Karma (Karma that obstructs power): Prevents the soul from exercising its inherent power, generating obstacles and impediments in spiritual practice and in the performance of meritorious actions.

Aghatiya Karmas, on the other hand, are non-obstructive Karmas, which affect the external conditions of the soul's life, such as the body, lifespan, social circumstances and pleasure/suffering, but do not directly obstruct its intrinsic faculties. There are also four main types of Aghatiya Karma:

Vedaniya Karma (Karma that causes experience): Responsible for the experiences of pleasure and suffering, generating pleasant and unpleasant sensations.

Ayu Karma (Karma that determines lifespan): Defines the lifespan in each incarnation, determining the period of existence in a given body.

Nama Karma (Karma that defines individuality): Responsible for the formation of the physical body, its characteristics, abilities and predispositions, conferring individuality and form to each being.

Gotra Karma (Karma that determines social status): Defines the social circumstances of birth, family, caste, wealth and social position, influencing the living environment and the opportunities available.

The mechanisms of binding (Bandha), fruition (Vedana), shedding (Nirjara) and liberation (Moksha) of Karma describe the cycle of accumulation, experience and elimination of karmic substance in the soul. Bandha (binding) is the process by which Karma adheres to the soul in response to actions, thoughts and intentions. The binding of Karma is influenced by several factors, such as the intensity of emotions (Kashaya), the nature of the action (Yoga), the modality of the action (Karana) and the cause of the action (Adhikarana). Actions driven by intense passions, such as anger, hatred, attachment and pride, generate a denser and more lasting Karma, while actions motivated by compassion, detachment and wisdom generate a lighter and more transient Karma.

Vedana (fruition) is the process of experiencing the results of accumulated Karma. Just as a planted seed germinates and produces fruit, Karma matures over time and manifests as experiences of pleasure and suffering, health and illness, success and failure, and other vicissitudes of life. The fruition of Karma is not a divine punishment or an arbitrary reward, but rather the natural and inevitable consequence of the law of spiritual cause and effect.

Nirjara (shedding) is the process of eliminating or "burning" accumulated Karma, releasing the soul from its influence. There are two main forms of Nirjara: Savipaka Nirjara (spontaneous shedding) and Avipaka Nirjara (intentional shedding). Savipaka Nirjara occurs naturally over time, when Karma matures and is exhausted through fruition. Avipaka Nirjara, on the other hand, is an active and intentional process, which involves ascetic practice, meditation, repentance and ethical conduct, aiming to accelerate the elimination of Karma and purify the soul.

Moksha (liberation) is the ultimate goal of the Jain spiritual journey, the state of complete and permanent liberation from the cycle of reincarnation and the yoke of Karma. Moksha is achieved when all Karmas, both Ghatiya and Aghatiya, are completely eradicated from the soul. In this state, the soul manifests its pure and original nature, free from any obscuration or limitation, experiencing infinite knowledge, infinite perception, infinite bliss and infinite power. The liberated soul (Siddha) ascends to the top of the universe (Siddhashila) and remains in a state of eternal bliss and perfection.

Individual responsibility for actions and their karmic consequences is a fundamental principle of the Jain Theory of Karma. In Jainism, each individual is the sole architect of their own destiny, responsible for their actions, thoughts and intentions, and reaping the (karmic) fruits of their choices. There is no external agent, such as a God or a supernatural force, that determines the destiny of the soul. Each being is free to choose their actions and, therefore, is fully responsible for the karmic consequences that arise from those choices. This emphasis on individual responsibility gives great power and autonomy to the individual in their spiritual journey.

Finally, Karma as the engine of reincarnation and the spiritual journey reveals its central role in the Jain worldview. The law of Karma is the mechanism that drives the cycle of reincarnation (Samsara), keeping the soul trapped in the material world until it breaks free from the yoke of Karma. Virtuous actions (Punya Karma) generate positive results, such as rebirths in favorable conditions and pleasant experiences, while non-virtuous actions (Papa Karma) generate negative results, such as rebirths in unfavorable conditions and painful experiences. The Jain spiritual journey is, in essence, a journey of karmic purification, aiming to eliminate accumulated negative Karma and to avoid the accumulation of new negative Karma, until the soul becomes completely free from the karmic yoke and attains final liberation (Moksha).

In summary, the Theory of Karma in Jainism is a complex and sophisticated system that explains the law of spiritual cause and effect in a detailed and comprehensive way. By understanding the nature of Karma as a subtle substance, its different categories, the mechanisms of binding, fruition, shedding and liberation, and individual responsibility for actions, the Jain practitioner is empowered to tread the spiritual path with wisdom, discernment and determination, seeking the purification of the soul, the overcoming of suffering and the attainment of final liberation (Moksha). In the next chapter, we will explore the concepts of Jiva and Ajiva, the soul and the non-soul, in the Jain worldview, deepening our understanding of the nature of the soul and its relationship with the material world, in the context of the Theory of Karma.

Chapter 9
The Soul and the Non-Soul

At the heart of the Jain worldview lies a fundamental distinction that permeates its entire philosophy and practice: the dichotomy between Jiva (Soul) and Ajiva (Non-Soul). This ontological duality, although seemingly simplistic at first glance, unfolds into a complex web of concepts and categories that elucidate the nature of existence, the origin of suffering, and the path to liberation. Understanding the distinction between Jiva and Ajiva is essential to grasping the Jain view of the universe, the human soul, and the ultimate goal of spiritual life.

Jiva, in Jainism, refers to the individual, conscious, and eternal soul. It is the living, sentient, and thinking entity that animates all living beings, from humans to the smallest microorganisms. The fundamental characteristic of Jiva is consciousness (Chetana), the ability to know, perceive, feel, and experience. In Jainism, belief in the existence of the individual and eternal soul is axiomatic, an unquestionable starting point for all its philosophy and practice.

The soul (Jiva) is described as being inherently pure, luminous, and perfect, possessing intrinsic qualities such as infinite knowledge (Ananta Jnana), infinite perception (Ananta Darshana), infinite bliss (Ananta Sukha), and infinite energy (Ananta Virya). However, this original purity of the soul is obscured and imprisoned by matter (Ajiva) and Karma. The soul, in its conditioned state, is like a lamp covered in dust, whose light is obscured by impurities.

Ajiva, in turn, encompasses the categories of the non-soul, the non-conscious and non-living elements that constitute the material universe. While Jiva represents the principle of life and consciousness, Ajiva represents the principle of matter and inertia. Jainism categorizes Ajiva into five main substances:

Pudgala (Matter): Refers to all physical matter, both gross and subtle, that makes up the material world. It includes the five classical elements (earth, water, fire, air, and ether), as well as atoms, subatomic particles, and all forms of matter that we perceive through the senses. Pudgala is characterized by form, color, smell, taste, and touch, and is inherently non-conscious and inert.

Akasha (Space): Is the substance that provides space and location for all other Dravyas (substances). Akasha is infinite, limitless, and omnipresent, permeating the entire universe. It is divided into Lokakasha (Occupied Space), the region of the universe where Jivas and other Dravyas reside, and Alokakasha (Empty Space), the infinite region beyond Lokakasha, which is devoid of Dravyas.

Kala (Time): Is the substance that enables change, duration, and the sequence of events. Time, in Jainism, is conceived as cyclical and eternal, divided into cosmic cycles of ascent and decline (Utsarpini and Avasarpini). Kala is measured in infinitesimal units of time (Samaya) and larger units such as hours, days, years, and cosmic eras.

Dharma (Principle of Motion): Does not refer to Dharma in the sense of "law" or "teaching," but rather to a unique substance that aids the movement of Jivas and Pudgalas. Dharma is omnipresent in Lokakasha, but passive and inert in itself. Just as water enables the movement of fish, Dharma enables the movement of Jivas and Pudgalas in space.

Adharma (Principle of Rest): Similar to Dharma, Adharma does not refer to "non-Dharma" or "injustice," but rather to a substance that aids the rest of Jivas and Pudgalas. Adharma is also omnipresent in Lokakasha and inert in itself. Just as the shade of a tree enables the rest of those seeking shelter, Adharma enables the rest of Jivas and Pudgalas in space.

The interaction between Jiva and Ajiva is at the heart of conditioned experience and karmic bondage. Although Jiva and Ajiva are distinct substances and opposite in nature (consciousness vs. non-consciousness), they interact continuously in the material world, giving rise to the phenomenon of life and suffering. Karmic bondage (Bandha) occurs when the soul (Jiva) associates with matter (Pudgala) through actions, thoughts, and intentions driven by passions and disturbing emotions (Kashayas). This interaction results in the accumulation of Karma in the soul, obscuring its original purity and imprisoning it in the cycle of reincarnation.

The process of karmic bondage is compared to the mixing of milk and water. Just as water mixes with milk and becomes difficult to separate, Karma mixes with the soul, obscuring its intrinsic qualities and creating a conditioned identity. This conditioned identity, driven by Karma, leads the soul to experience the cycle of birth, death, and rebirth, seeking illusory pleasures in the material world and suffering the consequences of its karmic actions.

The quest for the liberation of Jiva from the influence of Ajiva is the central goal of Jain practice. The path to liberation (Moksha) involves the purification of the soul from the influence of matter and Karma, through the practice of Ahimsa, asceticism, meditation, and self-discipline. By gradually eliminating accumulated Karma and avoiding the accumulation of new Karma, the soul becomes progressively purer and more luminous, manifesting its intrinsic qualities of infinite knowledge, perception, bliss, and power.

The Jain view of the interconnectedness of all beings and elements of the universe emerges from understanding the relationship between Jiva and Ajiva. Although Jiva and Ajiva are distinct categories, they are interconnected and interdependent in the context of conditioned experience. All living beings, possessing Jiva, share the same fundamental nature of consciousness and the same quest for liberation from suffering. The elements of Ajiva, such as matter, space, time, motion, and rest, provide the setting and means for the manifestation of life and conditioned experience. This interconnected view promotes a sense of universal responsibility and a deep respect for all forms of life and the environment.

In summary, the distinction between Jiva and Ajiva is a fundamental pillar of the Jain worldview, elucidating the dual nature of conditioned existence. Jiva, the conscious and eternal soul, seeks to free itself from the influence of Ajiva, the material and non-conscious world, through karmic purification. Understanding this duality and the interaction between Jiva and Ajiva is crucial to treading the Jain spiritual path, seeking liberation from the cycle of suffering and the realization of the true nature of the soul. In the next chapter, we will explore in detail the concept of Bondage and Liberation (Moksha), the ultimate goal of Jainism, unveiling the path to the purification of the soul and the attainment of eternal bliss.

Chapter 10
Bondage and Liberation

In the vast and intricate tapestry of Jainism, a shimmering golden thread weaves through every doctrine, practice, and precept: the relentless pursuit of Liberation (Moksha). This sublime, transcendental state is the pinnacle of the Jain spiritual journey, the ultimate and supreme goal towards which all efforts, aspirations, and renunciations converge. Moksha represents the complete and permanent liberation from the cycle of birth, death, and rebirth (Samsara), the definitive extinction of all suffering, and the full manifestation of the soul's true nature in its original purity and perfection. To understand the essence of Jainism, it is imperative to delve into the depths of the concept of Moksha, unveiling the state of bondage that precedes it, the arduous path that leads to it, and the indescribable bliss that characterizes it.

The starting point for understanding Moksha is the recognition of the state of bondage (Bandha), the condition in which the soul (Jiva) currently finds itself, imprisoned by karmic impurities. As explored in the previous chapter, the soul, in its intrinsic nature, is pure, luminous, and perfect. However, due to its interaction with the material world (Ajiva) and the accumulation of

Karma, this original purity is obscured and distorted. Bandha represents this karmic prison, the state in which the soul is bound to the cycle of Samsara, subject to suffering and impermanence.

Karmic bondage is not an external imposition or a divine punishment, but rather a self-created consequence of the soul's own actions, thoughts, and intentions. Driven by disturbing passions and emotions (Kashayas), the soul engages in activities that generate Karma, like a magnet attracting iron particles. These karmic particles, in turn, obscure the soul's faculties, creating veils of ignorance, attachment, aversion, and illusion, which keep it trapped in the cycle of Samsara. Bandha is, therefore, a state of self-enslavement, where the soul is trapped by the chains of its own Karma.

Suffering (Dukha) is the inevitable consequence of the state of karmic bondage. In Jainism, suffering is recognized as a fundamental reality of conditioned existence. It is not just the obvious physical or emotional suffering, but a deep existential dissatisfaction, a sense of incompleteness, impermanence, and lack of peace that permeates all experiences of the cycle of Samsara. This suffering (Dukha) arises from the very nature of conditioned existence, which is characterized by impermanence (Anitya), the absence of lasting substance (Anatma), and the source of dissatisfaction and pain (Dukkha).

Suffering (Dukha) as a result of karmic bondage manifests in countless ways in everyday life. From physical pain and illness, to emotional and mental anguish, through losses, disappointments, frustrations, and the very inevitability of old age, sickness, and death, suffering permeates all stages of conditioned existence. Jainism recognizes that suffering is not just an individual experience, but a universal condition shared by all living beings trapped in the cycle of Samsara. This understanding of the universality of suffering motivates the search for liberation and compassion for all suffering beings.

The path of liberation (Moksha), in Jainism, is an arduous, gradual, and multifaceted journey that involves the purification of the soul from all karmic impurities and the manifestation of its true nature. This path is outlined by the Three Jewels (Ratnatraya): Right View, Right Knowledge, and Right Conduct, and is followed through the rigorous practice of Jain vows, asceticism, meditation, and self-discipline. The central objective of the path of liberation is the shedding (Nirjara) of all accumulated Karma and the prevention of the accumulation of new Karma.

The purification of the soul on the path of Moksha involves both the elimination of negative Karma (Papa Karma) and positive Karma (Punya Karma). Although positive Karma can generate rebirths in more favorable conditions and more pleasant experiences, it still keeps the soul trapped in the cycle of Samsara and prevents complete liberation. Therefore, the ultimate goal is not only to accumulate positive Karma, but to eradicate all types of Karma, both good and bad, to achieve the state of absolute purity and liberation.

The state of liberation (Moksha) is described as a state of perfection, bliss, and infinite freedom. In this state, the soul is completely freed from the cycle of reincarnation and all forms of suffering. Moksha is not a physical place or a heavenly paradise, but a state of being, a radical transformation of consciousness, where the soul fully manifests its intrinsic qualities of infinite knowledge, infinite perception, infinite bliss, and infinite power. It is a state of unwavering peace, serenity, and joy, free from any form of pain, suffering, or imperfection.

In the state of Moksha, the soul is no longer subject to Karma, nor to the influence of the material world (Ajiva). It transcends the limitations of time, space, and causality, reaching a state of eternity, omniscience, and omnipotence in its own nature. The liberated soul (Siddha) resides in a state of transcendental bliss, free from any need or desire, in perfect harmony with itself and the universe. Moksha is the state of supreme realization, the ultimate goal of the Jain spiritual journey, and the promise of a future of peace and freedom for all beings.

The characteristics of the liberated Jiva (Siddha) reveal the magnificence and fullness of the state of Moksha. A liberated Jiva, a Siddha, possesses four infinite qualities (Ananta Chatushtaya):

Infinite Knowledge (Ananta Jnana): The Siddha possesses perfect and complete knowledge of everything that exists, past, present, and future, in all universes. Its knowledge is free from any obscuration or limitation.

Infinite Perception (Ananta Darshana): The Siddha possesses perfect and unlimited perception of all objects and events, at all times and places. Its perception is clear, sharp, and free from any distortion or illusion.

Infinite Bliss (Ananta Sukha): The Siddha experiences unwavering happiness and bliss that transcends any worldly pleasure or joy. Its bliss is intrinsic to its own pure nature and does not depend on external factors.

Infinite Energy (Ananta Virya): The Siddha possesses unlimited power and energy, although it does not use it to interfere in the material world or exert control over other beings. Its energy is directed towards maintaining its state of perfection and bliss.

In addition to these four infinite qualities, the Siddha is also described as possessing other characteristics, such as the absence of physical form, immortality, omnipresence (in the sense of not being limited by space), and complete freedom from suffering and imperfection. The Siddhas reside in Siddhashila, the top of the universe, in a state of eternal bliss and contemplation, serving as inspiring examples for those who are still treading the path of liberation.

In conclusion, Bondage and Liberation (Bandha and Moksha) represent the opposite poles of the Jain spiritual journey. Bandha, the state of karmic imprisonment and suffering, is the initial condition of the conditioned soul. Moksha, the state of complete liberation and bliss, is the ultimate and supreme goal. The Jain path, outlined by the Three Jewels and practiced through asceticism and self-discipline, aims at the transition from Bandha to Moksha, the purification of the soul, and the realization of its maximum potential.

Moksha is not just a distant and abstract goal, but a real and tangible possibility, a future of peace, freedom, and bliss that awaits those who sincerely dedicate themselves to the Jain path of liberation. In the next chapter, we will explore the ascetic and spiritual practices that constitute the core of the path to Moksha, such as fasting, meditation, and self-discipline, unveiling the Jain methods for purifying the soul and achieving liberation.

Chapter 11
Asceticism and Spiritual Practice

On the arduous and rewarding path of the Jain spiritual journey, asceticism emerges as an essential tool, a set of rigorous and transformative practices designed to purify the soul of karmic impurities and propel the practitioner towards liberation (Moksha). Asceticism, known in Jainism as Tapas, is not conceived as self-imposed suffering or a form of self-punishment, but rather as a strategic and conscious method to weaken the dominance of Karma over the soul, strengthen self-discipline, and cultivate intrinsic spiritual qualities. Through various forms of ascetic practices, such as fasting, meditation, and self-discipline, the Jain seeks to refine the mind, control the senses, and tread the path of karmic purification with determination and purpose.

The role of asceticism (Tapas) in karmic purification is central to Jain practice. As explored in previous chapters, Karma is conceived as a subtle substance that adheres to the soul and keeps it trapped in the cycle of reincarnation. Asceticism acts as a purifying fire, capable of "burning" or "dissolving" accumulated Karma, releasing the soul from its weight and obscuration. Ascetic practice, when performed with the correct intention and under proper guidance, generates a process of Nirjara (shedding), accelerating the elimination of Karma and facilitating spiritual progress.

There are different forms of asceticism in Jainism, encompassing both physical and mental practices, adapted to the capacities and path of each practitioner. Some of the most common forms of Jain asceticism include:

Fasting (Anasana): Fasting is a fundamental ascetic practice in Jainism, practiced in various forms and durations. It can range from complete fasting from food and water for a determined period (sometimes several days), to more moderate forms, such as fasting from certain types of food, restricting the amount of food, or practicing eating only once a day. Fasting aims to purify the body, reduce sensory desires, strengthen self-discipline, and generate spiritual merit.

Food Restriction (Unodarika): In addition to complete fasting, Jainism also emphasizes the importance of moderation and restriction in eating in general. This includes avoiding overeating, consuming luxurious or indulgent foods, and practicing strict vegetarianism, avoiding foods that involve violence or animal suffering. Food restriction aims to control the desires of the palate, cultivate contentment, and avoid attachment to sensory pleasures.

Silence (Mauna): The practice of silence, or Mauna, is another important form of Jain asceticism. It can involve complete verbal silence for a determined period, or restricting speech to only the essential, avoiding idle, futile, or harmful conversations. Silence aims to calm the mind, reduce mental dispersion, cultivate introspection, and avoid negative Karma generated by careless or violent speech.

Meditation (Dhyana): Meditation is a central practice in Jainism, both as a form of asceticism and as a means to achieve self-awareness and liberation. The practice of meditation (Dhyana) to calm the mind and achieve self-awareness is multifaceted and encompasses various techniques and methods, which we will explore in greater detail below.

Self-Discipline (Samyama): Self-discipline, or Samyama, permeates all forms of Jain asceticism and is a fundamental principle in itself. It refers to the control of the senses, mind, and passions, through the practice of constant vigilance, moderation, and self-sufficiency. Self-discipline aims to strengthen the will, overcome negative habits, cultivate virtues, and direct energy towards spiritual practice.

The practice of meditation (Dhyana) occupies a prominent place in Jain asceticism and is considered an essential means for purifying the mind, developing self-awareness, and achieving liberation. Jain meditation is not limited to a single technique or method, but encompasses a variety of contemplative practices, which aim to calm the agitated mind, focus attention, cultivate concentration, and achieve deeper states of consciousness.

An important form of Jain meditation is Samayika, the daily practice of meditation and introspection, recommended for both monks and nuns, and laymen and laywomen. Samayika generally involves a fixed period of time (for example, 48 minutes), during which the practitioner retreats to a quiet place, assumes a meditative posture, and focuses the mind on an object of meditation, such as the breath, Jain teachings, or the nature of the soul. Samayika aims to cultivate mental presence, reduce mental dispersion, and strengthen the connection with the Dharma.

Another important Jain meditative practice is Pratikramana, the daily ritual of repentance and confession of ethical and moral transgressions committed throughout the day. Pratikramana involves reflecting on the actions, words, and thoughts of the day, recognizing faults, sincere repentance, and the commitment to avoid repeating them in the future. Pratikramana aims to purify the mind of moral impurities, strengthen ethical awareness, and cultivate self-transformation.

Jainism also emphasizes the practice of Dhyana in its deepest senses, as advanced forms of meditation that aim to achieve higher states of consciousness and the direct experience of the nature of the soul. These forms of Dhyana can involve techniques of intense concentration, visualization, contemplation, and self-inquiry, seeking to transcend the dualistic mind, overcome attachment to the ego, and realize union with pure and infinite consciousness.

The importance of self-discipline (Samyama) to control the senses and passions is a recurring theme in Jain asceticism. It is believed that the senses and passions are the main sources of attachment to the material world and the accumulation of Karma. Self-discipline (Samyama) is the antidote to this tendency, enabling the practitioner to master sensory impulses, control disturbing emotions, and direct energy towards spiritual practice. Self-discipline encompasses all aspects of life, from eating and sleeping to speech, behavior, and relationships. It is a continuous process of vigilance, effort, and self-transformation, aiming to refine the mind, strengthen the will, and cultivate inner freedom.

Finally, Jainism recognizes the importance of finding a balance between asceticism and daily life for laymen and laywomen. While Jain monks and nuns dedicate themselves entirely to radical ascetic practice, laymen and laywomen, who live in the world and have family and professional responsibilities, are encouraged to practice asceticism in a way adapted to their life context. The Anuvratas (minor vows) offer a practical guide for Jain ethics in lay life, encouraging the practice of non-violence, truthfulness, non-stealing, chastity, and non-possessiveness within the possibilities and limitations of everyday life. In addition, laymen and laywomen are encouraged to practice periodic fasting, daily meditation, the study of scriptures, and other ascetic practices that they can integrate into their routines, seeking gradual and constant spiritual progress. Jainism values both the radical ascetic path of monks and nuns and the adapted ascetic path of laymen and laywomen, recognizing that both can lead to the purification of the soul and liberation, depending on the sincerity, effort, and intention of the practitioner.

In summary, asceticism and spiritual practice are intrinsic and indispensable elements of Jainism.

Through Tapas, the Jain practitioner seeks to purify the soul, eliminate Karma, strengthen self-discipline, and cultivate the spiritual qualities necessary for liberation. Fasting, food restriction, silence, meditation, and self-discipline are some of the ascetic tools used to refine the mind, control the senses, and tread the path of karmic purification. Jainism offers a comprehensive and flexible ascetic path, adapted for both monks and nuns and laymen and laywomen, inviting everyone to embark on the journey of self-transformation and the pursuit of inner peace and spiritual liberation. In the next chapter, we will explore the Fourteen Stages of Spiritual Development (Gunasthanas), the map of the Jain spiritual journey, which describes the different levels of purification and progress towards liberation, providing a detailed guide for ascetic and spiritual practice.

Chapter 12
The Path of Purification

To guide the practitioner on the intricate journey of spiritual purification, Jainism offers a detailed and comprehensive map: the Fourteen Stages of Spiritual Development, known as Gunasthanas. These stages represent a gradual and ascending progression in the soul's journey towards liberation (Moksha), outlining the different levels of purity, knowledge, and moral conduct that the practitioner can achieve along the ascetic path. The Gunasthanas are not mere descriptive categories, but rather a practical and dynamic guide, which helps the Jain to understand their own spiritual state, to identify the obstacles to be overcome, and to direct their efforts towards the advancement to the final goal. Exploring the Fourteen Gunasthanas is like unveiling a detailed roadmap of the soul's journey, revealing the challenges, achievements, and transformations that mark the Jain path of purification.

The Gunasthanas, as a map of the Jain spiritual journey, provide a valuable framework for self-understanding and spiritual progress. The word "Gunasthana" can be translated as "place of qualities" or "stage of virtues," indicating that each stage represents a specific level of development of spiritual qualities and a corresponding decrease of karmic impurities. The Fourteen Gunasthanas are arranged in an ascending sequence, from the first to the fourteenth, reflecting a linear progress in the soul's journey towards liberation. Although progression through the Gunasthanas is not always continuous and linear, the map offers a clear reference for evaluating one's own spiritual state and directing practice.

The initial stages of ignorance and delusion (Mithyatva Gunasthanas) comprise the first four Gunasthanas, characterized by a distorted view of reality, the lack of faith in Jain principles, and the predominance of disturbing passions and emotions. These stages represent the spiritual condition of most ordinary human beings, who live immersed in ignorance, attachment to the material world, and the cycle of suffering.

First Gunasthana: Mithyatva (Falsehood): This is the lowest stage, characterized by complete ignorance of the Jain truth and belief in distorted views of reality. The individual in this stage has no Right View (Samyak Darshana), does not understand the nature of the soul, Karma, liberation, or the Jain path. They are completely immersed in the material world, seeking sensory pleasures and living under the dominion of disturbing passions and emotions.

Second Gunasthana: Sasadana (Degradation): This stage represents a brief lapse in Right View for those who have already attained it. The individual in this stage experiences a temporary fall from their Jain faith and knowledge, usually due to the influence of intense passions or unfavorable circumstances. However, this stage is transitory and the individual usually returns to Right View soon.

Third Gunasthana: Mishra (Mixed): In this stage, the individual experiences a mixture of Right View and distorted view. There is an initial awakening to the Jain truth, but there is still a dose of doubt, confusion, and attachment to non-Jain beliefs. The individual may have moments of clarity and faith, followed by moments of doubt and hesitation.

Fourth Gunasthana: Avirata Samyaktva (Right View with Minor Vows): This stage marks the beginning of the true Jain spiritual journey, with the awakening of Right View (Samyak Darshana). The individual in this stage acquires a firm faith in Jain principles, understands the nature of the soul, Karma, and liberation, and aspires to follow the Jain path. Although they have not yet completely renounced worldly life and do not practice the Great Vows, they adopt the Anuvratas (minor vows) for laymen and laywomen, beginning to refine their ethical and moral conduct.

The intermediate stages of awakening and moral progress (Avirati and Virati Gunasthanas) comprise the Gunasthanas from the fifth to the tenth, marking a significant advance in the spiritual journey, with the development of ethical and moral conduct and the practice of self-discipline and asceticism. In these stages, the individual strives to purify their mind, control their senses, and advance towards the complete eradication of Karma.

Fifth Gunasthana: Deshavirati (Partial Vows): This stage represents the beginning of monasticism for those who take the step of renouncing lay life and joining the Jain monastic community. The individual in this stage adopts the Mahavratas (Great Vows), but only partially, not in their most complete and rigorous form. There are still certain weaknesses and imperfections in their practice, but there is a sincere commitment to the ascetic path.

Sixth Gunasthana: Pramatta Virati (Perfect Vows with Negligence): In this stage, the monk or nun practices the Mahavratas completely and rigorously, but still occasionally experiences lapses of negligence or carelessness. Disturbing passions and emotions can still arise occasionally, leading to minor transgressions of the vows. However, there is a constant effort to maintain ethical and moral conduct and to progress in ascetic practice.

Seventh Gunasthana: Apramatta Virati (Perfect Vows without Negligence): This stage marks a significant advance in self-discipline and mental control. The monk or nun practices the Mahavratas perfectly and vigilantly, without negligence or carelessness. Disturbing passions and emotions are greatly weakened and the mind becomes calmer and more focused on spiritual practice.

Eighth Gunasthana: Apoorva Karana (New Thought): In this stage, the monk or nun begins a process of intense and unprecedented karmic purification. A new type of thought and intention arises, focused exclusively on the eradication of Karma and the pursuit of liberation. There is a significant increase in spiritual energy and ascetic determination.

Ninth Gunasthana: Anivrutti Karana (Unchanging Thought): In this stage, the intention to eradicate Karma becomes even stronger and more stable. The mind becomes almost completely free of distractions and passions, focused exclusively on spiritual practice and the pursuit of liberation. Progress in karmic purification accelerates significantly.

Tenth Gunasthana: Sukshma Samparaya (Subtle Passion): In this stage, almost all passions and disturbing emotions have been eradicated, except for the most subtle and tenuous passion: subtle attachment. This residual passion is extremely difficult to detect and eliminate, but it still prevents complete liberation. The monk or nun in this stage is very close to the final goal, but still needs to overcome this last obstacle.

The advanced stages of purification and eradication of Karma (Kshapak and Upashamak Shreni) comprise the Gunasthanas from the eleventh to the thirteenth, representing the apex of the ascetic journey, with the complete eradication of passions and the attainment of perfect knowledge and liberation. These stages are accessible only to exceptional human beings, who have attained a level of extraordinary purity and self-discipline.

Eleventh Gunasthana: Upashanta Moha (Suppressed Passion): In this stage, all passions and disturbing emotions, including subtle attachment, are temporarily suppressed or subdued. The mind becomes completely calm and peaceful, experiencing a deep and serene bliss. However, this state of suppression is not permanent and passions can resurface, leading to a fall to a lower stage.

Twelfth Gunasthana: Kshina Moha (Eradicated Passion): In this stage, all passions and disturbing emotions, including subtle attachment, are completely eradicated and eliminated forever. The mind becomes absolutely pure and transparent, free from any obscuration or disturbance. The individual in this stage attains Kevala Jnana (Perfect Knowledge), the supreme enlightenment, becoming a Tirthankara or an enlightened being.

Thirteenth Gunasthana: Sayoga Kevali (Kevali with Activity): This is the stage of the enlightened Jinas or Tirthankaras, who have attained Kevala Jnana, but still remain in physical form, teaching the Dharma and guiding other beings on the path of liberation. They possess perfect knowledge, perfect perception, perfect bliss, and perfect power, but are still subject to certain physical and mental activities, such as breathing, eating, and preaching.

The final stage of complete liberation (Siddha Gunasthana) is the Fourteenth Gunasthana:

Fourteenth Gunasthana: Ayoga Kevali (Kevali without Activity): This is the last stage of physical existence, reached by Tirthankaras and other enlightened beings shortly before their physical death. In this stage, all physical and mental activities cease completely, including breathing and thinking. The individual becomes totally absorbed in the bliss of Nirvana, preparing for final and permanent liberation.

After physical death in this stage, the soul is completely freed from the body and the cycle of reincarnation, attaining Moksha (Liberation), the state of eternal perfection and bliss, becoming a Siddha, a liberated being.

The importance of understanding the Gunasthanas for spiritual self-improvement lies in its value as a practical guide for the journey of soul purification. By studying and contemplating the Gunasthanas, the Jain practitioner can:

Evaluate their own spiritual state: Identify which stage of spiritual development they are in, recognizing their strengths and weaknesses, their achievements and challenges.

Identify the obstacles to be overcome: Understand which passions, karmic impurities, and negative habits need to be combated and transformed in order to advance to the next stage.

Direct spiritual practice: Adapt their ascetic and spiritual practices to the specific needs of their current stage, focusing on the aspects of ethical conduct, meditation, self-discipline, and knowledge that are most relevant to their progress.

Cultivate motivation and hope: Visualize progression through the Gunasthanas as a real and achievable path towards liberation, strengthening faith, determination, and perseverance in spiritual practice.

The Fourteen Gunasthanas, therefore, are not just an abstract philosophical theory, but a practical and inspiring map for the Jain spiritual journey. They offer a detailed roadmap for the purification of the soul, overcoming suffering, and achieving final liberation (Moksha), inviting each practitioner to embark on this transformative journey with wisdom, discernment, and hope. In the following chapters, we will explore Jain practices and lifestyle, unveiling how the principles and stages of spiritual development manifest in the daily lives of Jain practitioners, both monks and nuns and laymen and laywomen.

Chapter 13
Jain Monasticism

In the multifaceted panorama of Jainism, monasticism emerges as a central and revered institution, representing the ultimate ideal of spiritual practice and the most direct and dedicated path towards liberation (Moksha). The Jain monastic community, composed of monks (Sadhu) and nuns (Sadhvi), is the backbone of the tradition, the guardian of the teachings, the embodiment of ascetic values, and the beacon that guides laymen and laywomen on their spiritual journey. Within this monastic ideal, however, different interpretations and practices have flourished throughout history, culminating in the formation of the two main sects of Jainism: Digambara and Svetambara. Understanding the nuances and distinctions between these two monastic traditions is fundamental to appreciating the richness and complexity of Jainism in its entirety.

The two main sects of Jainism, Digambara (sky-clad) and Svetambara (white-clad), represent the major divisions within the Jain tradition, diverging in certain aspects of doctrine, ascetic practice, and scriptures. The split between the two sects is traditionally attributed to historical events that occurred a few centuries after the death of Mahavira, related to issues of monastic practice and interpretation of the teachings. Although they share the fundamental principles of Jainism, such as Ahimsa, Karma, Moksha, and reverence for the Tirthankaras, Digambaras and Svetambaras have developed distinct monastic traditions, reflecting different emphases and approaches to ascetic practice and the spiritual journey.

The differences and similarities in the monastic practices of the two sects are notable and revealing of the nuances within Jainism. The most visible and frequently mentioned distinctions reside in the practices related to clothing, possession of material goods, dietary practices, and views on the possibility of women attaining liberation.

Clothing, or the absence of it, is perhaps the most emblematic difference between the two sects. Digambara monks, faithful to their designation "sky-clad," practice the asceticism of nudity. They completely renounce all clothing, remaining naked as a symbol of total detachment from the material world and radical ascetic purity. This practice is seen as the highest form of non-possessiveness and self-discipline, representing an extreme challenge to social comforts and conventions. Digambara nuns, for reasons of social modesty, wear a simple, unstitched sari, but maintain the principle of maximum non-possessiveness in relation to clothing.

Svetambara monks and nuns, on the other hand, follow the tradition of wearing white, unstitched garments, hence the name "white-clad." They wear simple garments, usually two or three pieces of white cloth, such as a loincloth, a robe, and a cloth to cover the mouth (Muhapatti), which is used to avoid harming small organisms in the air when speaking. For the Svetambaras, the use of white garments is seen as compatible with asceticism, providing modesty and protection from the elements, without compromising the essential principle of non-possessiveness.

Regarding the possession of material goods, both sects emphasize the importance of non-possessiveness (Aparigraha) as a fundamental vow for monks and nuns. However, the interpretation and application of this vow differ between Digambaras and Svetambaras. Digambara monks take non-possessiveness to the extreme, possessing only the items absolutely essential for ascetic practice, such as a water pot, a peacock feather broom (Pinchi) to remove small living beings from the path, and the scriptures. They traditionally do not possess begging bowls, eating the food they receive directly in their hands.

Svetambara monks and nuns, although they also practice non-possessiveness, allow a slightly greater possession of material goods, considered necessary for monastic life and the study of the scriptures. In addition to white garments, they generally possess a begging bowl, a walking stick, a blanket, and copies of the sacred scriptures. For the Svetambaras, the main focus of non-possessiveness lies in mental and emotional detachment from material goods, rather than absolute physical deprivation.

Food and begging practices also reveal distinctions between the two sects. Both Digambaras and Svetambaras practice begging (Gochari) as a way of obtaining food, depending on the charity of laymen and laywomen to sustain their ascetic lives. However, Digambara monks follow a more restricted begging practice, traditionally accepting food only once a day, and only by hand, without using bowls or containers. They also avoid eating while standing or moving, and traditionally do not accept food prepared for them, but only unsolicited leftovers.

Svetambara monks and nuns follow a more flexible begging practice, accepting food in begging bowls, and may make several begging rounds a day, if necessary. They may also accept food prepared for them, as long as it is vegetarian and prepared according to Jain principles of non-violence. Both sects emphasize the importance of receiving food with detachment and gratitude, as a necessity to sustain the body and allow spiritual practice, and not as a source of pleasure or indulgence.

Views on women and liberation represent another significant doctrinal difference between Digambaras and Svetambaras. The Digambara tradition holds that women cannot attain liberation (Moksha) in female form. According to this view, the female form is considered inherently less conducive to radical ascetic practice and the complete eradication of Karma, due to the biological and social differences between men and women. To achieve liberation, a Digambara woman must be reborn as a man in a future life, to then practice radical asceticism and achieve Moksha. In Digambara monasticism, therefore, only men can become completely naked monks, while nuns follow a less radical ascetic path, with the ultimate goal of being reborn as men to achieve liberation.

The Svetambara tradition, on the other hand, does not impose gender restrictions for liberation. The Svetambaras believe that women are spiritually equal to men and have the same capacity to practice asceticism, purify the soul, and achieve Moksha in female form. Svetambara Jain history reports examples of enlightened nuns (Sadhvis) who achieved liberation in female form, such as Mallinatha, the 19th Tirthankara, who the Svetambara tradition believes to have been a woman. In Svetambara monasticism, both men and women can become monks and nuns, seeking liberation through ascetic practice, without the need to be reborn in a male form.

Finally, the scriptures and canons also diverge between Digambaras and Svetambaras, as mentioned in Chapter 4. The Svetambaras accept a complete Agama canon of 45 texts, which they believe preserve the original teachings of Mahavira. The Digambaras, in turn, believe that the original Agamas were lost, and that the texts currently available are of secondary authority. This divergence in the scriptural canons reflects the different histories and traditions of oral and written transmission that developed in the two sects over time.

Despite these significant differences, it is important to emphasize that similarities still link Digambaras and Svetambaras within the Jain Dharma. Both sects share the fundamental principles of Jainism, such as the Three Jewels, the Five Great Vows

(Mahavratas), the Theory of Karma, the pursuit of liberation (Moksha), and reverence for the Tirthankaras. Both monastic traditions are dedicated to the practice of Ahimsa, asceticism, meditation, and self-discipline, seeking the purification of the soul and spiritual progress. The differences between them can be seen as variations within the same central theme, different approaches to ascetic practice and the spiritual journey, maintaining the essence of the Jain Dharma.

In both traditions, the ideal of radical asceticism remains central to the pursuit of spiritual liberation. Both Digambaras and Svetambaras consider monastic life as the highest and most direct path to Moksha, emphasizing the importance of renunciation, self-discipline, and karmic purification. The differences in their ascetic practices can be interpreted as different degrees of emphasis on certain aspects of asceticism, but the ultimate goal remains the same: liberation from the cycle of suffering and the realization of the true nature of the soul.

In conclusion, Jain monasticism, with its diverse manifestations in the Digambara and Svetambara traditions, represents a fundamental pillar of the Jain tradition. The differences between these two sects, although visible in practices such as clothing, possession of goods, food, and views on women, do not obscure the essential unity of the Jain Dharma, which lies in the pursuit of liberation through ascetic practice and the purification of the soul. Both Digambaras and Svetambaras offer valid and inspiring paths for the spiritual journey, inviting practitioners to transcend the material world, cultivate non-violence, and walk the path towards inner peace and final liberation. In the next chapter, we will explore the specific Jain practices for laymen and laywomen, unveiling how Jain principles and values can be lived and practiced in the context of daily life, outside the monastic environment.

Chapter 14
Jain Practices for Laymen and Laywomen

While Jain monasticism represents the ultimate ideal of renunciation and ascetic practice, Jainism also offers a valuable and accessible path for laymen and laywomen, those who live in the world and maintain family and professional responsibilities. Recognizing that not everyone is called or able to follow the rigor of monasticism, Jainism provides a set of ethical practices and guidelines adapted to lay life, allowing laymen and laywomen to experience Jain principles in their daily lives, seeking gradual spiritual progress and virtuous living within society. At the heart of these practices for laymen and laywomen are the Anuvratas (minor vows), a mitigated version of the monastic Great Vows, and a set of additional ethical guidelines that guide the moral, social, and religious conduct of Jain practitioners in lay life.

The Anuvratas (minor vows) represent the adaptation of the Mahavratas (Great Vows) to the context of lay life, offering a practical guide for Jain ethics in everyday life. Just as the Mahavratas are the fundamental vows for monks and nuns, the Anuvratas are the essential vows for laymen and laywomen, allowing them to experience Jain principles in a realistic and sustainable way in their daily lives. There are five Anuvratas, corresponding to the Five Great Monastic Vows, but with a lessened level of rigor, suitable for the capabilities and responsibilities of lay life:

Ahimsa Anuvrata (Minor Non-Violence): Just as the Mahavrata of Ahimsa requires absolute non-violence in thought, word, and deed for monks and nuns, the Anuvrata of Ahimsa for laymen and laywomen requires a commitment to avoiding intentional and unnecessary violence in all its forms. Although laymen and laywomen may not be able to completely avoid the violence inherent in everyday life (for example, in professions, in food), they commit to minimizing violence in their actions as much as possible, avoiding intentionally harming other living beings, cultivating compassion and respect for all life. The Anuvrata of Ahimsa for laymen and laywomen also manifests itself in the practice of vegetarianism, as a way to reduce participation in violence against animals.

Satya Anuvrata (Minor Truth): The Mahavrata of Satya requires absolute truthfulness from monks and nuns. The Anuvrata of Satya for laymen and laywomen requires a commitment to avoiding gross and intentional lying, and to speaking the truth as best as possible, in a kind and beneficial way. Although laymen and laywomen may occasionally encounter situations where the "truth" needs to be mitigated for reasons of courtesy or to avoid greater harm, the Anuvrata of Satya encourages them to prioritize honesty and integrity in their communication, avoiding deceit, defamation, and harmful language.

Asteya Anuvrata (Minor Non-Stealing): The Mahavrata of Asteya requires complete abstention from stealing for monks and nuns. The Anuvrata of Asteya for laymen and laywomen requires a commitment to avoiding theft, fraud, and misappropriation of material or intellectual property that does not rightfully belong to them. Laymen and laywomen are encouraged to be honest in their business dealings, to pay their taxes, to respect the property of others, and to avoid any form of exploitation or illicit gain.

Brahmacharya Anuvrata (Minor Chastity): The Mahavrata of Brahmacharya requires absolute celibacy for monks and nuns. The Anuvrata of Brahmacharya for laymen and laywomen requires a commitment to marital fidelity and moderation in sexual activity. Laymen and laywomen are encouraged to be faithful to their partners, to avoid adultery, and to practice moderation in sensual pleasures, directing some of their energy towards spiritual practice and inner development. For single people, the Anuvrata of Brahmacharya may mean sexual abstinence or the practice of chastity to different degrees, depending on their capabilities and aspirations.

Aparigraha Anuvrata (Minor Non-Possessiveness): The Mahavrata of Aparigraha requires complete detachment from material goods for monks and nuns. The Anuvrata of Aparigraha for laymen and laywomen requires a commitment to limiting possessiveness and attachment to material goods, practicing generosity and contentment. Laymen and laywomen are encouraged to avoid greed, excessive consumerism, and the unnecessary accumulation of wealth. They are encouraged to share their resources with those in need, to practice charity, and to live with simplicity and contentment, recognizing that true happiness does not reside in material possessions, but rather in inner peace and purity of soul.

In addition to the Anuvratas, there are additional ethical guidelines for laymen and laywomen that complement the minor vows and offer a more detailed guide for Jain life in everyday life. These guidelines include practices such as:

Diksha (Additional Vows): Laymen and laywomen may choose to take additional vows (Diksha) beyond the Anuvratas, to strengthen their spiritual practice and deepen their commitment to the Jain Dharma. These additional vows may include stricter dietary restrictions (such as avoiding certain foods or practicing longer fasts), the regular practice of meditation (Samayika), the study of scriptures (Agama Adhyayana), visiting Jain temples (Derasar), and other ascetic and devotional practices.

Samayika (Daily Meditation): The practice of daily meditation (Samayika) is strongly encouraged for Jain laymen and laywomen. Setting aside time daily for meditation, even for a short period, helps to calm the mind, cultivate self-awareness, and strengthen the connection with the Dharma. Meditation can be practiced in different forms, such as focusing on the breath, contemplating Jain teachings, reciting mantras, or practicing mental stillness.

Proshadhopavas (Periodic Fasting): The practice of periodic fasting (Proshadhopavas), usually once or twice a month, is another important ethical guideline for Jain laymen and laywomen. Periodic fasting, even for a day or half a day, helps to purify the body and mind, strengthen self-discipline, and generate spiritual merit. Laymen and laywomen can adapt the practice of fasting to their capabilities and health conditions, choosing the form and duration of fasting that best suits their needs.

Atithi-Samvibhag (Sharing with Ascetics): The practice of Atithi-Samvibhag, which means "sharing with ascetic guests," is an ethical guideline that emphasizes the importance of supporting the Jain monastic community through the donation of food, clothing, and shelter. Laymen and laywomen are encouraged to offer hospitality and sustenance to Jain monks and nuns, recognizing the value of their ascetic path and the importance of preserving the monastic tradition. This practice also aims to cultivate generosity and detachment in laymen and laywomen, by sharing their resources with those who have renounced the material world.

Participation in Jain Rituals and Festivals: Laymen and laywomen are encouraged to actively participate in Jain rituals and festivals held in temples (Derasar) or in Jain communities. Participation in rituals such as Puja (worship), Aarti (offering of light), and festivals such as Mahavir Jayanti (Mahavira's birthday) and Paryushan Parva (festival of forgiveness) strengthens the connection with the Jain community, nurtures faith and devotion, and provides opportunities for group spiritual practice.

The role of the layman and laywoman in sustaining the Sangha and practicing the Dharma is crucial to the vitality and continuity of the Jain tradition. While monks and nuns dedicate themselves entirely to ascetic practice and the preservation of the teachings, laymen and laywomen play a fundamental role in the material and social support of the Sangha, offering financial support, food, clothing, and shelter to the ascetics, and creating a social environment conducive to the practice of the Dharma. This relationship of interdependence and mutual support between the monastic community and the lay community is a distinctive feature of Jainism, ensuring that the tradition is preserved and transmitted to future generations.

The pursuit of an ethical and virtuous life in the context of everyday life is at the heart of Jain practice for laymen and laywomen. The Anuvratas and ethical guidelines offer a practical roadmap for living according to Jain principles in the world, without the need to renounce family, professional, or social life. Jain laymen and laywomen seek to apply the values of Ahimsa, truth, non-stealing, chastity, and non-possessiveness in all their daily activities, in their relationships, in their businesses, in their consumption choices, and in their interactions with the environment. They strive to live consciously, responsibly, and compassionately, seeking the well-being of all beings and gradual spiritual progress on their journey towards liberation.

In summary, Jain practices for laymen and laywomen, centered on the Anuvratas and a comprehensive set of ethical guidelines, offer a valuable and accessible path to experiencing the Jain Dharma in the context of everyday life. These vows and guidelines provide a practical guide for moral, social, and religious conduct, allowing laymen and laywomen to cultivate non-violence, truth, non-stealing, chastity, and non-possessiveness in their daily lives, seeking gradual spiritual progress, virtuous living, and contributing to a more just, peaceful, and compassionate world. In the next chapter, we will explore the Jain diet and vegetarianism, unveiling the principles of Jain food as a fundamental expression of the principle of Ahimsa and an essential component of the Jain lifestyle for all practitioners, monks, nuns, laymen, and laywomen.

Chapter 15
The Jain Diet

In the multifaceted mosaic of the Jain tradition, diet takes on a significance that transcends mere physical nourishment, rising to a living and daily expression of the fundamental principle of Ahimsa (Non-Violence). The Jain diet, intrinsically linked to vegetarianism, is not just a food choice, but a deep ethical and spiritual commitment, a conscious practice that seeks to minimize to the greatest extent possible the violence and suffering inflicted on other living beings, even in the essential act of eating to sustain one's own life. Exploring the Jain diet is to unravel a unique and rigorous food system, guided by compassion, ecological responsibility and the pursuit of purification of the soul, offering an inspiring model for a more ethical and conscious diet in the contemporary world.

Vegetarianism as an expression of Ahimsa is the ethical foundation of the Jain diet. As we have explored extensively, Ahimsa, non-violence in all its forms, is the cornerstone of Jain ethics. In this context, the vegetarian diet emerges as a practical and concrete application of Ahimsa in daily life, seeking to avoid any participation in the violence inherent in the production of meat and other animal products. For the Jain, consuming meat means contributing directly to the cycle of suffering and death inflicted on animals, living beings that, like humans, possess a soul (Jiva) and the ability to feel pain and fear. By opting for vegetarianism, the Jain seeks to align their food choices with the principle of Ahimsa, cultivating compassion and respect for all life.

The Jain diet is not only vegetarian, but vegan for the most rigorous ascetics and predominantly lacto-vegetarian for laymen and laywomen, with nuances and degrees of rigor that vary between different Jain sects and traditions. Jain veganism, practiced mainly by Digambara monks and nuns and by some Svetambara ascetics, completely excludes all animal products, including meat, fish, eggs, dairy products and honey. This practice aims to avoid any form of animal exploitation and to minimize violence in food as much as possible.

Jain lacto-vegetarianism, more common among laymen and laywomen and in the Svetambara tradition in general, allows the consumption of dairy products (milk, cheese, yogurt, etc.), but continues to exclude meat, fish and eggs. Even in Jain lacto-vegetarianism, there is a constant concern to ensure that dairy products are obtained ethically and non-violently, avoiding practices that cause suffering or excessive exploitation of animals. Some lacto-vegetarian Jains also avoid consuming honey, considering it a product of bee exploitation.

Jain dietary restrictions go beyond the exclusion of animal products, also covering certain types of vegetables and roots, depending on the tradition and the degree of ascetic rigor. Some Jain traditions, especially among the Digambaras, avoid the consumption of roots and tubers such as potatoes, carrots, radishes, onions, and garlic. This restriction is based on the principle of *Ekindriya Jiva Himsa*, non-violence to one-sensed beings. Roots and tubers are considered to have a greater potential for latent life and to harbor a greater number of microorganisms, and their harvesting is seen as involving a greater degree of violence and destruction of life forms. This restriction is more common among ascetics and less followed by laymen and laywomen, who generally consume a greater variety of vegetables.

The principles behind Jain dietary restrictions reflect the rigorous application of Ahimsa and the pursuit of minimizing violence in food. The main principles that guide the Jain diet include:

Ahimsa (Non-Violence): As a central principle, Ahimsa motivates the exclusion of meat, fish and eggs, and the maximum reduction of the consumption of animal products, aiming to avoid violence and suffering inflicted on animals.

Karuna (Compassion): Compassion for all living beings motivates the choice of a diet that causes the least possible harm and suffering to other creatures. The Jain diet seeks to reflect compassion in every meal, recognizing the interconnectedness of all life.

Aparigraha (Non-Possessiveness): The principle of Non-Possessiveness is reflected in the simplicity and moderation of the Jain diet. Avoiding luxurious, indulgent or overly processed foods, and opting for simple, natural and nutritious foods, aligns with the principle of detachment and contentment.

Samyama (Self-Discipline): The Jain diet requires self-discipline and control of sensory desires, especially the palate. Restricting certain types of food and practicing periodic fasting are ways to strengthen self-discipline and refine the mind, directing energy towards spiritual practice.

Viveka (Discernment): Discernment and wisdom guide Jain food choices. Understanding the karmic consequences of actions, including food choices, and discerning between foods that promote physical and spiritual health and those that harm it, is essential for the practice of the Jain diet.

Practical implications of the Jain diet in daily life cover various aspects of everyday life, from the choice of foods and the preparation of meals to social behavior and eating out. In choosing food, the conscious Jain seeks to prioritize vegetarian foods, preferably vegan, fresh, natural and minimally processed. Reading labels, questioning the origin of food and opting for products of ethical and sustainable origin are common practices.

In the preparation of meals, the Jain diet encourages simplicity, moderation and care in the preparation of food, avoiding waste and excessive consumption of energy and resources. Cooking with compassionate intention, in a clean and peaceful environment, and offering food as an offering before eating are devotional practices.

In social behavior and eating out, the Jain faces the challenge of maintaining their diet in a world that often does not understand or respect Jain dietary restrictions. Gently explaining their food choices, looking for vegetarian or vegan options in restaurants and social events, and bringing their own food when necessary are common strategies. Flexibility and adaptation are important, always maintaining the commitment to the ethical principles of Ahimsa and compassion.

Benefits of the Jain diet for physical, mental and spiritual health are recognized both by the Jain tradition and by modern science. From the point of view of physical health, the Jain diet, rich in vegetables, fruits, whole grains and legumes, and restricted in saturated fats, cholesterol and processed foods, can contribute to the prevention of chronic diseases such as heart disease, type 2 diabetes, certain types of cancer and obesity. Studies have shown that vegetarians and vegans tend to have a healthier body mass index (BMI), lower cholesterol levels and a lower risk of developing these diseases.

From the point of view of mental health, the Jain diet, by promoting moderation, simplicity and contentment, can contribute to emotional and mental well-being. The practice of mindful eating, gratitude for food and the reduction of attachment to sensory pleasures can calm the mind, reduce stress and cultivate inner peace.

From the point of view of spiritual health, the Jain diet is seen as an essential means for the purification of the soul and spiritual progress. By aligning food choices with the principles of Ahimsa and compassion, the Jain strengthens their ethical practice, accumulates spiritual merit and advances towards liberation (Moksha). The Jain diet is not just a way to nourish the body, but also a continuous spiritual practice, an act of devotion and a path to self-transformation.

Finally, the relevance of the Jain diet in the modern world resonates with increasing urgency in a global context marked by ethical, environmental and health concerns related to food production and consumption. In a world where meat and dairy production contributes significantly to greenhouse gas emissions, deforestation, water pollution and large-scale animal exploitation, the Jain diet offers a more sustainable and compassionate food model, aligned with the values of environmental responsibility and animal ethics.

Furthermore, in a world where diet-related chronic diseases are one of the main causes of morbidity and mortality, the Jain diet, rich in whole plant foods, offers a path to a healthier and more preventive diet, promoting physical well-being and longevity. The Jain diet, therefore, is not just an ancient religious practice, but a relevant and inspiring food model for the 21st century, an invitation to rethink our food choices, to cultivate compassion and responsibility, and to build a more ethical, healthy and sustainable future for all living beings.

In summary, the Jain diet and vegetarianism represent a deep and comprehensive expression of the principle of Ahimsa in everyday life. Much more than a simple dietary restriction, the Jain diet is an ethical and spiritual commitment, a path to the purification of the soul, integral health and the contribution to a more compassionate and sustainable world. By exploring the principles, practices and benefits of the Jain diet, we can be inspired to rethink our own food choices, to cultivate compassion on the plate and to tread a path of more ethical, conscious and responsible eating, for the benefit of ourselves, other living beings and the planet. In the next and final chapter, we will explore the contemporary relevance of Jainism, revealing how Jain principles and values can be applied and experienced in the modern world, facing the challenges and opportunities of the 21st century.

Chapter 16
Jain Temples and Rituals

In the multifaceted landscape of the Jain tradition, temples (Derasar) and rituals play a crucial role, offering sacred spaces for worship, devotion, and spiritual practice, and serving as vibrant centers of the Jain community. These places of worship, richly imbued with symbolism and meaning, are not mere buildings, but rather portals to transcendence, spaces where the Jain practitioner can connect with the Tirthankaras, cultivate faith and devotion (Bhakti), and deepen their journey towards liberation (Moksha). Exploring Jain temples and rituals is to enter the beating heart of Jain devotional practice, unveiling the richness of its symbolism, the beauty of its ceremonies, and the importance of its community and cultural function.

The architecture and symbolism of Jain temples (Derasar) reflect the core values and principles of Jain philosophy, such as Ahimsa (non-violence), purity, serenity, and the pursuit of transcendence. Jain temples, known as Derasar (Gujarati term) or Mandir (Hindi term), are generally built following specific architectural principles, with distinctive features that differentiate them from other Indian religious temples.

The basic structure of a Derasar generally includes:

Garbhagriha (Inner Sanctum): The heart of the temple, where the main image of the Tirthankara (Murtis) is installed. It is the most sacred space of the temple, reserved for the most important rituals and for the presence of the priests (Pujari).

Gudhamandapa (Assembly Hall): A spacious hall in front of the Garbhagriha, where devotees gather for prayers, chants, and religious discourses. The Gudhamandapa can be richly decorated with carved pillars, domes, and paintings.

Mukhamandapa (Entrance Porch): A porch or veranda at the entrance of the temple, which serves as a transition space between the outside world and the sacred space of the temple.

Shikhar (Spire or Tower): A tall and elaborately carved tower, which rises above the Garbhagriha, marking the presence of the temple and serving as a visual focal point.

Manastambha (Column of Honor): A tall and imposing column, usually located in front of the temple, adorned with sculptures and Jain symbols. The Manastambha symbolizes the refutation of pride and the humble entry into the temple.

The symbolism present in Jain architecture is profound and multifaceted. The eastern orientation of most temples symbolizes the pursuit of enlightenment, which arises with the rising sun. The elaborate sculptures and ornamental motifs represent the beauty and perfection of the Jain universe, and the multiplicity of living beings. The images of the Tirthankaras in the Garbhagriha represent the enlightened beings, the ideal models of spiritual perfection, and the guides on the path of liberation. The atmosphere of peace and serenity that permeates Jain temples aims to create an environment conducive to introspection, meditation, and devotion.

The images of the Tirthankaras (Jinas) are the central objects of veneration in Jain temples. The Tirthankaras, the "Ford-Makers", are enlightened human beings who have attained liberation (Moksha) and who, out of compassion, teach the path of liberation to other beings. There are 24 Tirthankaras in each cosmic cycle, with Rishabhanatha being the first and Mahavira the last Tirthankara of the current cycle.

The images of the Tirthankaras (Murtis) are idealized representations of these enlightened beings, characterized by a serene and contemplative expression, conveying peace, calm, and absence of passions. The Murtis are generally represented in two main postures:

Kayotsarga (Posture of Abandonment of the Body): An erect posture, with the arms straight along the body or slightly apart, representing standing meditation and detachment from the physical body. This posture symbolizes radical asceticism and renunciation of the material world.

Padmasana (Lotus Posture): A seated posture with the legs crossed in lotus, representing seated meditation and the state of balance and inner harmony. This posture symbolizes mental tranquility and spiritual stability.

The Murtis of the Tirthankaras are generally made of stone, marble, or metal, and can be nude (Digambara) or dressed with simple adornments (Svetambara), reflecting the different monastic traditions. The Murtis are not seen as deities in the theistic sense, but rather as inspiring symbols of Jain ideals, representing the human potential to achieve spiritual perfection and liberation. Venerating the Murtis is not about seeking favors or blessings, but rather cultivating devotion (Bhakti), drawing inspiration from the examples of the Tirthankaras, and strengthening one's own spiritual journey.

The daily rituals and ceremonies in Jain temples are devotional practices that aim to express reverence for the Tirthankaras, purify the mind and body, and strengthen the connection with the Dharma. Some of the most common rituals and ceremonies include:

Puja (Worship): Puja is a daily ritual of worship to the Tirthankaras, which can be performed individually or in a group, in the temple or at home. Puja involves the symbolic offering of eight substances (Ashtamangala) to the Murtis of the Tirthankaras, representing the different aspects of the spiritual journey: water (purity), sandalwood (purity), flowers (non-violence), incense (fragrance), lamp (knowledge), rice (purity), fruits (liberation), and sweets (bliss). During Puja, devotees recite mantras, chants, and prayers, expressing their devotion and gratitude to the Tirthankaras.

Aarti (Offering of Light): Aarti is a ceremony of offering light, usually performed at dawn and dusk in

Jain temples. During Aarti, priests (Pujari) or devotees offer lighted lamps (lamps, candles) to the Murtis of the Tirthankaras, accompanied by chants, music, and prayers. Aarti symbolizes the dissipation of the darkness of ignorance and the illumination of spiritual knowledge.

Abhisheka (Anointing): Abhisheka is a ritual of anointing the Murtis of the Tirthankaras with water, milk, sandalwood, saffron, and other purifying substances. Abhisheka is performed on special occasions, such as festivals and consecration ceremonies of new Murtis, symbolizing the purification and revitalization of the sacred images.

Stavana (Prayer and Devotional Singing): Stavana refers to prayers, hymns, and devotional chants in praise of the Tirthankaras, which are recited individually or in a group, in temples or at home. Stavanas express devotion (Bhakti), gratitude, and admiration for the Tirthankaras, seeking inspiration in their examples and strengthening faith and connection with the Dharma.

The importance of devotion (Bhakti) and prayer (Stavana) in Jain practice lies in its role as a means of cultivating faith, humility, concentration, and spiritual connection. Although Jainism is not a theistic tradition in the conventional sense, devotion to the Tirthankaras and the practice of rituals and prayers are considered valuable practices on the path of soul purification. Jain Bhakti is not a form of worship of a creator God, but rather an expression of reverence and admiration for enlightened beings, seeking inspiration in their examples and strengthening one's own aspiration for liberation.

Devotion and prayer help to calm the mind, reduce selfishness and attachment, and cultivate spiritual qualities such as compassion, gratitude, and humility.

Finally, Jain temples as centers of community, education, and cultural preservation play a multifaceted role in Jain life, going beyond being just places of worship. Derasar serve as meeting points for the Jain community, where practitioners gather for rituals, festivals, religious discourses, social events, and community activities. The temples also function as centers of religious education, offering classes, lectures, courses, and study programs on Jain philosophy, ethics, scriptures, and practices, for children, youth, and adults. In addition, Jain temples act as guardians of Jain culture, preserving the art, architecture, literature, ritual traditions, and values of the Jain community, transmitting them to future generations.

In summary, Jain temples and rituals represent an essential dimension of the Jain tradition, offering sacred spaces for worship, devotion, spiritual practice, and community life. The architecture and symbolism of the temples reflect Jain values, while the images of the Tirthankaras inspire faith and the pursuit of liberation. Daily rituals and ceremonies, such as Puja, Aarti, Abhisheka, and Stavana, cultivate devotion, purification, and spiritual connection. Jain temples, more than mere buildings, are vibrant centers of community, education, and cultural preservation, playing a multifaceted role in the lives of Jain practitioners and in the continuity of the Jain tradition over the centuries. In the next chapter, we will explore Jain art and architecture in greater detail, unveiling the symbolism and distinctive aesthetics of Jain visual culture.

Chapter 17
Jain Art and Architecture

Jain art and architecture constitute a unique and inspiring visual treasure, eloquently and enduringly reflecting Jain values, philosophy, and worldview. Far from the exuberance or drama of other religious artistic traditions, Jain art is characterized by a serene, balanced, and harmonious aesthetic, imbued with deep and intentional symbolism. From the majestic sculptures of the Tirthankaras to the intricate details of the temples, Jain visual culture conveys a message of peace, non-violence, self-discipline, and the pursuit of liberation, inviting the observer to contemplation, introspection, and connection with the Dharma. Exploring Jain art and architecture is like deciphering a rich and complex visual language, revealing the essence of the Jain tradition and its unique contribution to the cultural heritage of India and the world.

The characteristics of Jain art reveal a distinctive aesthetic, shaped by the fundamental principles of Jainism. Jain art is not intended to adorn or entertain, but rather to inspire, educate, and spiritually elevate the observer. Some of the most striking features of Jain art include:

Emphasis on Peace and Serenity: Jain art seeks to convey an atmosphere of inner peace, calm, and serenity. The facial expressions of the Tirthankaras in the sculptures, the soft and harmonious colors in the paintings, and the balanced architecture of the temples contribute to creating an environment that invites contemplation and meditation.

Non-Violence (Ahimsa) as a Central Theme: The principle of Ahimsa permeates all Jain art, manifesting itself in the peaceful representation of beings, the absence of violent or aggressive scenes, and the choice of materials and techniques that minimize harm to other life forms. Jain art celebrates life, compassion, and respect for all living beings.

Idealization of the Human Form: The representations of Tirthankaras and other spiritual figures in Jain art are highly idealized, seeking to express spiritual perfection and the absence of passions. The figures are generally represented with harmonious proportions, serene facial features, and bodies devoid of excessive adornments, conveying an image of purity, self-discipline, and detachment.

Rich and Intentional Symbolism: Jain art is full of symbols that represent philosophical concepts, ethical principles, and spiritual qualities important in Jainism. Each element of Jain art, from the postures of the figures to the ornamental motifs and the colors used, has a deep symbolic meaning, which invites interpretation and reflection.

Detail and Precision: Jain art often demonstrates a high level of detail and precision in execution, reflecting the importance of careful attention, diligence, and perfection in Jain spiritual practice. The intricate elaboration of the sculptures, the fine and precise lines in the paintings, and the meticulously planned architecture of the temples bear witness to the care and dedication of Jain artists.

The representations of Tirthankaras in sculptures and paintings are the most revered and recurrent images in Jain art. As we have already explored, Tirthankaras are enlightened beings who have achieved liberation and teach the path of the Dharma. The artistic representations of the Tirthankaras serve as objects of veneration and inspiration, reminding practitioners of the ideals of spiritual perfection and the human potential to achieve liberation.

Sculptures of Tirthankaras are found in temples, home altars, and Jain pilgrimage sites. Generally made of stone, marble, metal, or wood, the sculptures vary in size, from small portable statuettes to immense monumental images. The sculptures follow a rigorous iconographic canon, with standardized characteristics that identify the Tirthankaras and express their spiritual attributes:

Meditative Postures: Sculptures generally represent Tirthankaras in Kayotsarga (standing posture) or Padmasana (lotus posture), symbolizing meditation, asceticism, and spiritual stability.

Individual Symbols (Lanchhana): Each Tirthankara is associated with a specific animal symbol (Lanchhana), which distinguishes him from the others. For example, Rishabhanatha is associated with the bull,

Ajitanatha with the elephant, and Mahavira with the lion. The Lanchhana is usually carved on the base of the statue or on other decorative elements.

Shrivatsa: A spiral or diamond-shaped symbol engraved on the chest of the Tirthankaras, representing the pure and infinite soul.

Three Umbrellas (Chattra Traya): Three umbrellas above the statue's head, symbolizing the Tirthankaras' spiritual dominion over the three worlds (celestial, terrestrial, and infernal).

Halo (Prabhavali): A circular halo or aura around the statue's head, representing the aura of light and knowledge that emanates from the Tirthankaras.

Jain paintings, in turn, are found in illustrated manuscripts, temple panels, murals, and other forms of art. Jain paintings use a palette of soft and earthy colors, with an emphasis on shades of red, yellow, green, and blue, creating a calm and harmonious atmosphere. The paintings often depict scenes from the lives of the Tirthankaras, narratives from Jain scriptures, cosmological diagrams (Lokapurusha), and symbolic representations of Jain principles. The traditional Jain painting technique, especially in illustrated manuscripts, is known for its precision of lines, minute details, and vibrant colors, applied with natural inks derived from minerals, plants, and organic pigments.

The use of Jain symbols is a striking feature of Jain art and architecture, giving them a deep and multifaceted meaning. Some of the most important and recurring Jain symbols include:

Swastika: One of the most auspicious and universal symbols of Jainism, the Swastika (not to be confused with the Nazi swastika, which is an inversion of the Jain symbol) represents the four states of existence that the soul can experience in the cycle of reincarnation: celestial, human, infernal, and non-human (animal or plant). The four arms of the Swastika can also represent the Four Gems of Dharma: Right Knowledge, Right Faith, Right Conduct, and Right Asceticism.

Shri Vatsa: Already mentioned, the Shri Vatsa, in the shape of a spiral or diamond on the chest of the Tirthankaras, symbolizes the pure and infinite soul, the essence of liberated consciousness.

Nandavarta: A nine-pointed star-shaped diagram or square mandala, representing Mount Meru, the central cosmic mountain of the Jain universe, and the different levels of Jain cosmology.

Darpana (Mirror): The mirror symbolizes the pure and immaculate soul, which reflects reality without distortion. It can also represent self-awareness and the importance of reflecting on one's own actions and thoughts.

Kalasha (Sacred Vessel): The vessel filled with water, often represented in Jain temples, symbolizes fullness, prosperity, and purity. It can also represent the nectar of immortality and the pursuit of liberation.

Twin Fish (Matsyayugala): Two fish side by side, swimming in opposite directions, symbolize the cycle of birth and death (Samsara) and the duality of conditioned existence. They can also represent the search for balance and overcoming duality.

The architecture of Jain temples is characterized by a variety of elements and styles, which vary according to the region, historical period, and Jain sect. However, some architectural elements are common to most Jain temples, reflecting the principles and values of the tradition:

Pillars (Stambha): Jain temples often feature richly carved pillars, supporting the roofs, domes, and mandapas. The pillars can be decorated with figures of deities, geometric motifs, floral patterns, and narratives from Jain scriptures. The pillars symbolize the stability, support, and strength of the Dharma.

Domes (Shikhar): As mentioned, the Shikhar, the pinnacle or tower that rises above the Garbhagriha, is a distinctive feature of Jain temples. The domes can vary in shape and size, but are generally elaborately carved and adorned, symbolizing spiritual ascension and the pursuit of liberation.

Mandapas (Halls): The Mandapas, the halls for gathering and prayer, are large and open spaces, designed to accommodate devotees and the temple's community activities. The Mandapas can be decorated with pillars, sculptures, paintings, and windows that allow natural light to enter, creating an airy and welcoming environment.

Toranas (Ornamental Arches): The Toranas, richly carved entrance arches, mark the entrance to the temple or to sacred areas within the temple. The Toranas can be adorned with figures of Yakshas and Yakshinis (protective deities), animals, geometric patterns, and narratives from Jain scriptures, symbolizing the entry into the sacred space and the transition to the spiritual world.

Jali (Perforated Stone Screens): In some Jain temples, especially in the architectural styles of western India, the windows and walls can be constructed with Jali, perforated stone screens with intricate geometric or floral patterns. The Jali allow light and ventilation to enter, while maintaining privacy and creating a visual effect of light and shadow.

Jain art and architecture, as expressions of Jain philosophy and values, transcend mere visual aesthetics, becoming powerful vehicles for the transmission of the teachings of the Dharma. By contemplating the sculptures of the Tirthankaras, the Jain symbols, and the architecture of the temples, the Jain practitioner is reminded of the ideals of non-violence, self-discipline, purity, and the pursuit of liberation. Jain art not only decorates sacred spaces, but also imbues them with spiritual meaning, creating an environment conducive to devotion, meditation, and inner transformation. Jain visual culture, with its serene beauty and profound symbolism, offers a valuable contribution to the artistic and spiritual heritage of humanity, inviting reflection on the eternal values of peace, compassion, and the pursuit of truth. In the next chapter, we will explore Jain festivals and celebrations, unveiling the main religious festivities and how the Jain community celebrates and experiences the Dharma through the festive calendar.

Chapter 18
Main Religious Festivals

The Jain calendar is punctuated by a series of festivals and celebrations that mark important religious dates, honor revered figures, and strengthen the community spirit of the Jain Sangha. These festivals, vibrant in color, devotion, and meaning, are not mere festive occasions, but rather spiritual opportunities to deepen the practice of Dharma, renew vows, seek purification of the soul, and celebrate the core values of Jainism. Exploring Jain festivals is to delve into the vibrant rhythm of Jain religious life, unveiling the traditions, rituals, and deep spiritual significance that permeate these festive dates.

Mahavir Jayanti, the celebration of the birth of Mahavira, the last Tirthankara of the current cycle, is one of the most important and revered festivals in the Jain calendar. Celebrated annually on the thirteenth day of the dark fortnight of the month of Chaitra (usually in March or April), Mahavir Jayanti commemorates the birth of Vardhamana, who would later become Mahavira, the great reformer and propagator of Jainism. On this auspicious day, Jains celebrate the life, teachings, and legacy of Mahavira, renewing their commitment to Jain principles and seeking inspiration from his example of asceticism, non-violence, and the pursuit of liberation.

The celebrations of Mahavir Jayanti vary in detail among different Jain sects and regions, but generally include common elements such as:

Visits to Temples (Derasar): Jains traditionally visit temples (Derasar) on Mahavir Jayanti to offer prayers, participate in rituals, and venerate the Murtis (images) of Mahavira and other Tirthankaras. The temples are specially decorated and illuminated for the occasion, creating a festive and devotional atmosphere.

Abhisheka (Ritual Anointing): In many temples, Abhisheka is performed, the ritual of anointing the Murtis of Mahavira with water, milk, and other purifying substances. This ritual symbolizes the purification and revitalization of the spiritual energy of the sacred images.

Processions and Parades: In some Jain cities and communities, festive processions and parades are organized on Mahavir Jayanti, with the Murti of Mahavira being carried on a palanquin or carriage through the streets, accompanied by devotional songs, music, and dances.

Readings of Scriptures (Agama): Religious speeches and readings of Jain scriptures (Agama) are held in temples and community centers on Mahavir Jayanti, recalling the teachings of Mahavira and inspiring practitioners to follow the path of Dharma.

Donations and Charity (Dana): In the spirit of compassion and generosity, Jains practice charity and donations (Dana) on Mahavir Jayanti, offering food, clothing, money, and other assistance to those in need. Blood donation drives, food distribution to the poor, and community service events are common on this day.

Fasting and Ascetic Practices: Some Jains observe partial or complete fasting on Mahavir Jayanti, as a way of practicing asceticism and self-discipline, emulating the example of Mahavira. Meditation, prayer, and other spiritual practices are intensified on this day, seeking the purification of the soul and connection with the Dharma.

Paryushan Parva, known as the "festival of forgiveness" and the most important festival of the Jain year, is an eight-day period of intense spiritual practice, introspection, and repentance. Celebrated annually during the month of Bhadrapada (usually in August or September), Paryushan Parva offers Jains a valuable opportunity to reflect on their actions, words, and thoughts of the previous year, to seek forgiveness for any transgressions, and to renew their commitment to Jain principles.

The eight days of Paryushan Parva are marked by various spiritual practices, including:

Ayambil Tap: Many Jains practice Ayambil Tap during Paryushan, a type of rigorous fasting that allows eating only once a day, at a specific time, and only bland, uncooked foods. Ayambil Tap aims to purify the body, strengthen self-discipline, and reduce attachment to the pleasures of taste.

Upvas (Fasting): In addition to Ayambil Tap, many Jains also observe complete fasting (Upvas) for one or more days during Paryushan, abstaining from food and water. Fasting is seen as a powerful form of asceticism, purification, and introspection.

Pratikramana (Repentance and Confession): Pratikramana, the daily ritual of repentance and confession, is practiced in an intensified way during Paryushan. Jains reflect on their ethical and moral transgressions of the previous year, ask forgiveness from all living beings they may have harmed, and make vows to avoid repeating these mistakes in the future.

Reading of Scriptures (Kalpa Sutra): During Paryushan, Jain scriptures, especially the Kalpa Sutra, which narrates the life of the Tirthankaras, are read and explained in temples and community centers. The Kalpa Sutra is considered a sacred and inspiring text, and its reading during Paryushan aims to recall the teachings of Dharma and strengthen faith.

Religious Speeches (Pravachan): Jain monks and nuns deliver religious speeches (Pravachan) during Paryushan, addressing topics such as Ahimsa, Karma, Moksha, the importance of forgiveness, and spiritual practice. Pravachan offer guidance, inspiration, and clarification on Jain Dharma.

Kshamapana (Forgiveness Day): The last day of Paryushan, known as Samvatsari Pratikramana or Kshamavani, is dedicated to forgiveness. On this day, Jains actively seek forgiveness from all those they may have offended, and offer forgiveness to all who have offended them, through the traditional formula "Micchami Dukkadam" (which means "may all my transgressions be fruitless of uselessness"). Kshamapana aims to purify relationships, cultivate compassion, and promote social harmony.

Diwali (Deepavali), the festival of lights, although also celebrated by Hindus and Sikhs, has a special meaning for Jains, marking the date of Mahavira's liberation (Moksha). Celebrated on the last day of the month of Ashvin, Diwali, for Jains, is not only a festival of lights and celebration of prosperity, but rather a commemoration of Mahavira's enlightenment and liberation from the cycle of birth and death. On this day, Jains celebrate the triumph of the light of knowledge over the darkness of ignorance and Mahavira's attainment of Nirvana.

Jain Diwali celebrations include:

Nirvana Kalyanak Puja: A special Puja is performed in Jain temples on Diwali, known as Nirvana Kalyanak Puja, to celebrate Mahavira's Nirvana and venerate his liberated soul (Siddha). This Puja emphasizes the pursuit of liberation and the ideal of Moksha.

Illumination of Temples and Homes: As in other Indian traditions, Jains also illuminate their temples and homes with oil lamps (Diyas) and electric lights on Diwali. The lighting symbolizes the light of spiritual knowledge that Mahavira brought to the world and the hope of dispelling the darkness of ignorance.

Lakshmi Puja (Symbolic): Although the goddess Lakshmi is more prominent in the Hindu pantheon, some Jains also perform a symbolic form of Lakshmi Puja on Diwali, seeking prosperity and well-being for the coming year. However, the Jain emphasis on Diwali remains on the celebration of spiritual liberation and not on the pursuit of material wealth.

Sweets and Gifts: Exchange of sweets and gifts between family and friends is also a common practice in Jain Diwali, strengthening social and community ties.

Akshaya Tritiya, celebrated on the third day of the bright fortnight of the month of Vaishakha (usually in April or May), commemorates a significant event in the life of Rishabhanatha, the first Tirthankara of the current cosmic cycle. Akshaya Tritiya marks the day when Rishabhanatha ended his long period of asceticism and fasting, receiving food for the first time after his enlightenment (Kevala Jnana). This festival celebrates the importance of charity (Dana), compassion, and sustenance for Jain ascetics.

Akshaya Tritiya celebrations include:

Re-enactment of Rishabhanatha's First Meal: In some Jain temples and communities, a symbolic re-enactment of Rishabhanatha's first meal is performed, with a monk or devotee representing Rishabhanatha receiving food from laymen and laywomen. This re-enactment aims to recall the importance of supporting ascetics and cultivating gratitude for the opportunity to practice charity (Dana).

Offering of Sugarcane Juice: Traditionally, on Akshaya Tritiya, Jains offer sugarcane juice to ascetics and temples, in memory of the original food that Rishabhanatha received. Sugarcane juice symbolizes nourishment, sweetness, and purity.

Dana (Charity): Akshaya Tritiya is considered a particularly auspicious day for the practice of charity

(Dana) in all its forms. Jains are encouraged to make donations to temples, charities, ascetics, and people in need, seeking to accumulate spiritual merit and express compassion.

In addition to these main festivals, the Jain calendar includes other important dates and observances, such as:

Pancha Kalyanakas: Celebrations that mark the five auspicious events in the life of each Tirthankara: Chyavana (conception), Janma (birth), Diksha (renunciation), Kevala Jnana (enlightenment), and Nirvana (liberation). The Pancha Kalyanakas can be celebrated on specific dates for each Tirthankara or in collective festivals.

Rohini Vrata: A fasting vow observed by Jain women to seek marital happiness and family prosperity. It is observed in all lunar months, with fasting on the day of Rohini Nakshatra (constellation).

Shashwati Vrata: A perpetual fasting vow observed by some Jains, practicing intermittent fasting throughout their lives, on specific days of the lunar calendar.

Jain festivals and celebrations, as an expression of community life and the practice of Dharma, play a multifaceted role in the Jain tradition. They strengthen community ties, providing opportunities for Jains to come together, celebrate together, share faith, and strengthen their relationships. Festivals also serve as vehicles for religious education, transmitting the teachings of Dharma to new generations through rituals, speeches, readings, and educational activities. In addition, Jain festivals inspire spiritual practice, motivating practitioners to intensify their ascetic practices, renew their vows, reflect on their lives, and seek the purification of the soul. Jain celebrations, in their essence, are living expressions of Dharma, moments of joy, devotion, and spiritual renewal that enrich the Jain journey and strengthen the Jain community worldwide. In the next chapter, we will explore the Jain community and its social engagement, unveiling Jain contributions to society and the role of Jainism in promoting peace, non-violence, and social justice.

Chapter 19
The Jain Community

The Jain tradition, since its origins in Ancient India, has never been restricted to the realm of individual contemplation and isolated ascetic practice. On the contrary, the Jain community (Sangha) has always played a vital role, acting as a foundation for the preservation of the faith, the transmission of teachings, and the manifestation of Jain values in the social fabric. Actively engaged with the world around it, the Jain community has offered notable contributions to society over the centuries, in areas as diverse as philosophy, art, literature, science, and ethics, promoting peace, non-violence, and social justice. Exploring the Jain community and its social engagement is to unveil the active and altruistic face of Jainism, understanding how its values transcend the individual sphere and radiate outwards, positively transforming the world.

The structure of the Jain community (Sangha) is a fundamental pillar of the tradition, constituting the backbone that sustains the Jain faith and practice throughout the generations. The Jain Sangha, traditionally divided into four parts - monks (Sadhu), nuns (Sadhvi), laymen (Shravaka), and laywomen (Shravika) - functions as a network of mutual support, learning, and spiritual practice, ensuring the continuity and vitality of the Jain Dharma.

The role of the Sangha in preserving the tradition is multifaceted and essential. Monks and nuns, fully dedicated to the ascetic life, act as the guardians of the teachings, preserving the sacred scriptures (Agamas), transmitting the knowledge of Dharma through preaching and teaching, and personifying the Jain ideals of renunciation, non-violence, and self-discipline. Laymen and laywomen, in turn, play a crucial role in the material and social support of the Sangha, offering financial support, food, clothing, and shelter to the ascetics, and creating a social environment conducive to the practice and dissemination of Jain values. This symbiotic and mutually supportive relationship between the monastic community and the lay community ensures the continuity of the tradition and the transmission of Dharma to future generations.

The importance of Jain education and the transmission of values to new generations is a constant priority within the Jain community. Recognizing that the preservation of tradition depends on the education and engagement of future generations, the Jain community invests significantly in educational institutions, religious education programs, and cultural activities aimed at children, youth, and adults. Jain temples (Derasar) and community centers often offer Dharma classes, Jainology courses, scripture study programs, spiritual retreats, and fun and educational activities for children and youth, aiming to inculcate Jain values from childhood, strengthen religious identity, and prepare new generations to assume responsibility for the continuity of the tradition.

Jain contributions to philosophy, art, literature, science, and ethics are vast and profound, enriching the cultural heritage of India and the world. In philosophy, Jainism developed sophisticated logical and epistemological systems, such as Anekantavada (relativism) and Syadvada (conditional predication), which offer unique perspectives on the nature of reality, knowledge, and truth, promoting tolerance, dialogue, and understanding of the multiplicity of points of view. In art and architecture, as explored in the previous chapter, Jainism bequeathed majestic temples, serene sculptures, and intricate paintings, imbued with deep symbolism and a distinctive aesthetic, conveying the values of peace, non-violence, and the pursuit of liberation. In literature, the Agamas and other Jain scriptures, preserved in ancient languages such as Ardhamagadhi and Sanskrit, constitute a rich body of philosophical, ethical, narrative, and poetic texts, which explore the spiritual journey, Jain cosmology, and the principles of Dharma.

In the area of science, although Jainism did not develop a scientific tradition in the modern sense, its philosophical and ethical principles, such as Ahimsa and Anekantavada, have resonance with contemporary scientific concepts, such as ecology, quantum physics, and complexity theory, offering valuable insights for a more ethical, responsible science aligned with the vision of interconnection and interdependence of life. In ethics, the Jain contribution is undeniable and seminal, with the principle of Ahimsa (non-violence) as the cornerstone of a comprehensive and rigorous ethical system, which encompasses all forms of life and influences individual, social, and political conduct, promoting compassion, justice, and peace.

The social engagement of the Jain community in areas such as education, health, and animal welfare reflects the practical application of Jain values in everyday life and the pursuit of a more just and compassionate world. In education, Jain educational institutions, from primary schools to universities, offer quality education, combining the academic curriculum with moral and ethical education based on Jain principles, forming conscious, responsible, and virtuous citizens. In the area of health, Jain hospitals and clinics, often run by Jain charitable organizations, offer accessible and compassionate health services, often with an emphasis on holistic and preventive approaches, and with respect for the dignity and rights of patients. In animal welfare, the Jain community is a pioneer and exemplar, with a strong commitment to animal protection, strict vegetarianism, the promotion of ethical alternatives to animal exploitation, and the operation of shelters and sanctuaries for rescued animals.

The role of Jainism in promoting peace, non-violence, and social justice is a distinctive mark of the Jain tradition and a relevant contribution to the contemporary world. The principle of Ahimsa, taken to its ultimate consequences in Jainism, is not just an abstention from physical violence, but rather a comprehensive ethical imperative that permeates all aspects of life, from food choices and individual behavior to public policies and international relations. The Jain community, throughout history, has positioned itself as a voice in defense of peace, justice, and non-violence, promoting dialogue, tolerance, mutual understanding, and the peaceful resolution of conflicts, both at the interpersonal level and at the global level. In a world marked by violence, injustice, and inequality, Jainism offers an alternative path, a model of a peaceful and compassionate society, based on the principles of non-violence, responsibility, and the interconnection of all life.

In summary, the Jain community and its social engagement represent a vital and dynamic dimension of the Jain tradition. The Sangha, with its structure and interdependence between monks, nuns, and laypeople, ensures the preservation and transmission of Dharma. Jain education aims to form new generations imbued with Jain values. Jain contributions to philosophy, art, literature, science, and ethics enrich the cultural heritage of humanity. Social engagement in education, health, and animal welfare demonstrates the practical application of Jain principles in everyday life. The role of Jainism in promoting peace, non-violence, and social justice offers a path to a more compassionate and harmonious world. The Jain community, in its diversity and engagement, continues to be a beacon of hope and an agent of positive transformation in the contemporary world, radiating the eternal values of Jainism beyond its religious and cultural boundaries. In Part IV of this book, we will explore Jainism in the Modern World, deepening the analysis of the contemporary relevance of Jainism and its applications in areas such as science, environmentalism, peacebuilding, interreligious dialogue, and the challenges and opportunities faced by Jainism in the 21st century.

Chapter 20
Jainism and Science

In the 21st century, in a world increasingly shaped by advances in science and technology, the dialogue between ancient religious traditions and modern scientific knowledge becomes not only pertinent but essential. Jainism, with its rich philosophy and sophisticated ethics, offers a unique perspective in this dialogue, revealing remarkable points of convergence and valuable insights that can enrich both the scientific understanding of reality and the ethical application of scientific knowledge. Exploring the relationship between Jainism and science does not mean seeking scientific validation of Jainist doctrines, but rather identifying conceptual parallels, areas of compatibility, and potential contributions that each field can offer the other, promoting a more comprehensive and integrated view of the world and humanity's place in it.

The parallels between Jainist principles and modern scientific concepts emerge in several areas, revealing surprising affinities between an ancient wisdom and the discoveries of contemporary science. Although Jainism is not a scientific tradition in the modern sense, certain fundamental principles of Jainist philosophy resonate with scientific concepts and models, suggesting an underlying compatibility and a common ground for dialogue.

First, ecology and the principle of Ahimsa find a remarkable point of convergence. The Jainist view of Ahimsa (non-violence), which extends to all forms of life and recognizes the interconnectedness of all living beings (Jiva), echoes the fundamental principles of modern ecology. Ecology teaches us about the complexity of ecological networks, the interdependence of species, and the importance of biodiversity for the health of the planet. Similarly, Jainism emphasizes the interconnectedness of all life, the importance of respecting and protecting all living beings, and the need to live in harmony with nature. Both perspectives recognize that violence against nature, whether through overexploitation of natural resources, pollution, or habitat destruction, has negative consequences not only for the environment but also for humanity itself. Jainist Ahimsa, therefore, can be seen as a fundamental ethical principle for environmentalism, offering a solid philosophical basis for the protection of the planet and the pursuit of a sustainable future.

Second, modern physics, particularly quantum physics and the theory of relativity, and the principle of Anekantavada (relativism) present intriguing conceptual resonances. Anekantavada, the Jainist doctrine of the multiplicity of perspectives and the relativity of truth, postulates that reality is complex, multifaceted, and that no single perspective can fully capture it. This view echoes the complexity and paradoxical nature of reality revealed by modern physics. Quantum physics, for example, demonstrates that subatomic particles can behave both as waves and as particles, depending on the observer's perspective. Einstein's theory of relativity challenges the classical notions of space and time as absolute entities, showing that they are relative to the observer and their frame of reference. Just as Jainist Anekantavada recognizes the validity of multiple perspectives in understanding reality, modern physics reveals that reality itself is multifaceted and depends on the observer's perspective. Anekantavada, therefore, can be seen as a precursor epistemological approach, which anticipates the complexity and relativity of reality that modern science reveals.

Third, biology and the theory of Jiva can be explored for points of connection, although with caution and respect for the distinctions between the fields. The Jainist concept of Jiva, the individual, conscious, and eternal soul, present in all living beings, can be interpreted, from a secular perspective, as a reference to the life force, consciousness, or the complexity inherent in life. Although biological science does not validate the existence of the soul in the Jainist metaphysical sense, it recognizes the complexity and uniqueness of living systems, the presence of self-organizing processes, the ability to respond to the environment, and, at more complex levels, the manifestation of consciousness. The Jainist view of Jiva, therefore, can be seen as an ancient philosophical expression of an intuition about the vitality and uniqueness of life, which, in a way, resonates with the admiration and reverence for the complexity of life that we also find in modern biology.

It is crucial to note that this comparison does not seek to scientifically validate the Jainist belief in the soul, but rather to identify a point of dialogue and reflection on the nature of life and consciousness.

Ahimsa and environmental ethics become particularly relevant in the context of the global ecological crisis we face today. The Jainist view of interconnectedness and respect for all life offers a solid ethical basis for environmentalism and the search for sustainable solutions to environmental challenges. Jainism invites us to rethink our relationship with nature, to abandon the anthropocentric view that places human beings at the center of the universe, and to adopt a biocentric or ecocentric perspective, which recognizes the intrinsic value of all forms of life and the need to protect and preserve the planet's biodiversity. Jainist environmental Ahimsa implies reducing consumption, minimizing waste, opting for sustainable practices, protecting natural habitats, and respecting animal rights. In a world threatened by climate change, biodiversity loss, pollution, and predatory exploitation of natural resources, Jainist environmental ethics offers a valuable guide for action and a call for global ecological responsibility.

Anekantavada and the complexity of reality resonate with the growing scientific understanding that the world is complex, multifaceted, and that natural phenomena can rarely be explained by simplistic or linear models. Modern science, in various fields such as physics, biology, social sciences, and complexity theory, recognizes the importance of perspective, context, and interconnectedness in understanding reality. Jainist Anekantavada, by reminding us of the multiplicity of perspectives and the relativity of truth, can help us develop a more open, flexible, and tolerant mind in relation to the complexity of the world, both in the scientific field and in other domains of life. The Jainist perspective can encourage us to overcome dogmatism, reductionism, and binary thinking, and to adopt a more holistic, integrative, and dialogical approach in the pursuit of knowledge and in solving complex problems.

Jainism and the search for an ethical and responsible science point to the need to integrate ethical and spiritual values into scientific practice and the application of scientific knowledge. Jainism, with its emphasis on Ahimsa, compassion, non-possessiveness, and self-discipline, can offer a valuable ethical framework to guide scientific research, technological innovation, and the use of scientific knowledge for the well-being of humanity and the planet. A science ethically informed by Jainism would seek to minimize harm and suffering, promote justice and equity, respect the diversity of life, and prioritize the common good above private or commercial interests. The dialogue between Jainism and science can contribute to the development of a more humane, responsible, and sustainable science, which recognizes the limits of scientific knowledge, the importance of intellectual humility, and the need to consider the ethical and social implications of each scientific advance.

In conclusion, Jainism and science, although following distinct paths in the search for knowledge, reveal points of convergence and mutual insights that enrich our understanding of the world. Jainism offers an ethic of non-violence that resonates with the principles of ecology and a call for environmental responsibility. Anekantavada anticipates the complexity and relativity of reality revealed by modern physics. The philosophy of Jiva inspires a reflection on the nature of life and consciousness. The dialogue between Jainism and science can contribute to the development of a more ethical, responsible, and holistic science, and to a more integrated, compassionate, and sustainable worldview. It is important to emphasize that this dialogue does not aim to subject faith to reason or to scientifically validate religious beliefs, but rather to explore the rich intersections between ancient wisdom and modern knowledge, seeking a future in which science and spirituality can walk together towards a better world. In the next chapter, we will deepen the discussion on Jainist environmental ethics, exploring in detail the ecological relevance of the principle of Ahimsa.

Chapter 21
Jainism and Environmentalism

In a world facing unprecedented environmental challenges, from climate change to biodiversity loss and widespread pollution, the ancient wisdom of religious traditions can offer valuable insights and guidance for action. Jainism, with its central principle of Ahimsa (Non-Violence), emerges as a prophetic and relevant voice in the contemporary environmental debate, offering a profound and comprehensive ecological ethic capable of inspiring a radical transformation in our relationship with nature and the planet. Exploring Jainism and environmentalism is to unveil the ecological relevance of Ahimsa, understanding how this ancient ethical principle can provide a solid foundation for protecting the environment, promoting sustainability, and seeking a harmonious future for all living beings.

Ahimsa as a fundamental principle of Jain environmentalism constitutes the foundation of a uniquely profound and comprehensive ecological ethic. As we have reiterated, Jain Ahimsa is not limited to the absence of physical violence against human beings, but extends to all forms of life (Jiva), recognizing that every living being has a soul, the capacity to feel pain and suffering, and the right to life and well-being. This inclusive view of Ahimsa transcends the anthropocentrism common in many other ethical traditions, placing the protection of all life at the center of morality and action.

In the environmental context, Ahimsa manifests as an ethical imperative to avoid any form of violence against nature, whether through the predatory exploitation of natural resources, pollution, habitat destruction, species extinction, or any action that causes harm or suffering to ecosystems and the living beings that inhabit them. Jain environmentalism, therefore, is not just a matter of protecting the environment for human benefit, but rather an intrinsic commitment to non-violence, a natural extension of the principle of Ahimsa to the realm of nature, recognizing the interconnectedness of all beings and the importance of living in harmony with the natural world.

The protection of all life forms and the rejection of the exploitation of nature are logical corollaries of the principle of Ahimsa in the Jain environmental context. For the Jain, nature is not merely a set of resources to be exploited for human benefit, but rather a home shared by countless life forms, each with its own intrinsic value and right to exist. The predatory exploitation of nature, driven by greed, consumerism, and a lack of consideration for other living beings, is seen as a form of violence, a transgression of the principle of Ahimsa, and a source of suffering and imbalance for the planet.

Jainism rejects the anthropocentric view that places human beings at the center of creation and considers them superior to other life forms. Instead, it proposes a biocentric or ecocentric perspective, which recognizes the inherent value of all living beings, regardless of their usefulness to humans, and which emphasizes the importance of protecting and preserving the planet's biodiversity. The protection of forests, rivers, oceans, animals, plants, and microorganisms is not just a matter of environmental responsibility, but rather a moral imperative for the Jain, an expression of Ahimsa and universal compassion.

Jain ecological practices stem directly from the principle of Ahimsa and Jain environmental ethics, offering a practical guide to living more sustainably and compassionately. Some of the most relevant Jain ecological practices include:

Strict Vegetarianism and Veganism: As explored in Chapter 15, the Jain diet, centered on vegetarianism and, ideally, veganism, is a fundamental expression of Ahimsa in food. By avoiding the consumption of meat and other animal products, the Jain reduces their participation in the violence inherent in livestock production, which contributes significantly to deforestation, greenhouse gas emissions, water pollution, and large-scale animal exploitation. Jain vegetarianism, therefore, is an essential ecological practice that minimizes the environmental impact of food and promotes a more compassionate relationship with animals.

Conscious and Minimalist Consumption: The Jain principle of Aparigraha (Non-Possessiveness) translates into practices of conscious and minimalist consumption. The Jain is encouraged to reduce excessive consumption, avoid waste, choose durable, reusable, and ethically and sustainably sourced products. Unbridled consumerism, driven by greed and attachment to material goods, is seen as a source of violence against nature and social imbalance. Jain conscious consumption seeks simplicity, moderation, and contentment, aligning lifestyle with the principles of Ahimsa and sustainability.

Waste Reduction and Management: The concern for non-violence extends to waste management in Jainism. Practitioners are encouraged to reduce waste production, recycle, compost, and dispose of waste responsibly, minimizing the environmental impact of pollution and contamination. The principle of Ahimsa, in this context, implies avoiding violence against the environment through pollution and degradation of ecosystems, and seeking sustainable solutions for waste management.

Conscious Use of Natural Resources: Jainism emphasizes the conscious and responsible use of natural resources, such as water, energy, land, and minerals. Practitioners are encouraged to save water and energy, use renewable energy sources, protect the soil, and avoid wasting natural resources. The principle of Ahimsa, in this context, implies avoiding the predatory exploitation of natural resources and seeking ways of life that are sustainable in the long term, respecting the limits of the planet and the needs of future generations.

Promotion of Biodiversity and Nature Conservation: Jainism values biodiversity and the beauty of nature, recognizing the importance of protecting natural habitats, endangered species, and fragile ecosystems. Practitioners are encouraged to support nature conservation initiatives, participate in reforestation projects, protect wild animals, and promote environmental education. The principle of Ahimsa, in this context, implies defending the rights of nature, recognizing the intrinsic value of all life forms, and seeking a harmonious relationship with the natural world.

Jainism and the pursuit of a sustainable and harmonious future for the planet reflect an integrated and comprehensive worldview that recognizes the interconnectedness of all living beings and the need to build a more just, peaceful, and sustainable society. Jain environmental ethics offers a valuable guide for action in the context of the global ecological crisis, proposing a path of personal and social transformation based on the principles of Ahimsa, compassion, non-possessiveness, and wisdom.

Jainism invites us to rethink our values, habits, and lifestyle, to abandon unbridled consumerism, greed, and predatory exploitation, and to adopt a more compassionate, responsible, and sustainable perspective towards the planet and all its inhabitants. The pursuit of a sustainable future, from the Jain perspective, is not just a matter of technology or politics, but rather a profound ethical and spiritual transformation, which requires a change of consciousness, an expansion of compassion, and a sincere commitment to non-violence in all its forms.

In conclusion, Jainism and environmentalism meet in the principle of Ahimsa, an ethic of non-violence that extends to all life and the planet. Jain environmental ethics proposes the protection of all life forms, the rejection of the predatory exploitation of nature, and the adoption of ecological practices such as vegetarianism, conscious consumption, waste reduction, and the responsible use of natural resources. Jainism offers an inspiring vision for the pursuit of a sustainable and harmonious future, based on compassion, responsibility, and the interconnectedness of all life. In a world that cries out for solutions to the environmental crisis, Jain ecological wisdom offers a valuable and relevant path, inviting us to act with Ahimsa for the benefit of ourselves, other living beings, and the planet as a whole. In the next chapter, we will explore the role of Jainism in peacebuilding, unveiling how Jain principles can be applied in conflict resolution and the promotion of social harmony.

Chapter 22
Peacebuilding

In a world often plagued by conflict, violence, and division, Jainism's message of peace resonates with singular urgency and relevance. The Jain tradition, centered on the supreme principle of Ahimsa (Non-Violence), not only condemns violence in all its forms, but also offers a practical and transformative path to peacebuilding, both individually and collectively. Exploring Jainism and peacebuilding is to unveil the revolutionary potential of Ahimsa as a powerful tool for conflict resolution, understanding how its principles can be applied to promote harmony, justice, and peaceful coexistence in a fragmented world.

Ahimsa as a tool for interpersonal, social, and international conflict resolution represents the core of the Jain approach to peace. Far from being just a passive abstention from violence, Jain Ahimsa is an active and dynamic force, an ethical principle that can be applied constructively to transform conflict situations, restore relationships, and build bridges of understanding and cooperation. Ahimsa, in this context, is not only the absence of physical violence, but also the absence of verbal, mental, and emotional violence, seeking to eradicate the roots of conflict at all levels of human experience.

At the interpersonal level, applying Ahimsa in conflict resolution means responding to anger with calmness, hatred with love, and violence with non-violence. In situations of disagreement or confrontation, the Jain is encouraged to practice active listening, compassionate communication, and the search for peaceful solutions that respect the rights and needs of all parties involved. Avoiding harsh words, hasty judgments, and impulsive reactions is essential to de-escalate conflict and create a space for constructive dialogue and reconciliation.

At the social and community level, Ahimsa can be applied to resolve tensions, promote social justice, and build peaceful and inclusive communities. Jainism encourages intergroup dialogue, the promotion of equality and equity, the defense of human rights, and the fight against discrimination and injustice through non-violent means. Social action inspired by Ahimsa seeks to transform the social structures that generate violence and inequality, building a more just, compassionate, and harmonious society for all its members.

At the international level, the application of Ahimsa in conflict resolution involves seeking diplomatic solutions, promoting intercultural dialogue, and advocating for peace through non-violent means. Jainism rejects war as a legitimate means of resolving disputes, advocating negotiation, mediation, international cooperation, and bridge-building between nations as paths to lasting peace. The Jain vision of a peaceful world is based on the premise that violence begets more violence, and that only non-violence can break the cycle of conflict and suffering.

The importance of dialogue, mutual understanding, and empathy in the Jain approach to conflict lies in the conviction that most conflicts arise from lack of communication, misunderstanding, intolerance, and lack of compassion. Jainism emphasizes the need to cultivate empathy, to put oneself in the other's shoes, to understand their perspectives, their needs, and their sufferings, as a fundamental step towards the peaceful resolution of conflicts. The principle of Anekantavada (relativism), which recognizes the multiplicity of perspectives and the relativity of truth, is essential for interreligious and intercultural dialogue, encouraging tolerance, intellectual humility, and openness to listening and learning from others.

Jain dialogue seeks to create a safe and respectful space for open and honest communication, where all parties involved can express their opinions, feelings, and needs, without fear of judgment or violence. The goal of dialogue is not necessarily to reach complete consensus, but rather to promote mutual understanding, identify areas of agreement and disagreement, and find creative and peaceful solutions that are acceptable to all involved. Empathy, in the Jain context, is not just a passive feeling of sympathy, but rather an active capacity to connect with the experience of the other, to feel their pain and suffering as if they were one's own. Empathy motivates compassionate action, the pursuit of justice, and non-violent conflict resolution, aiming to alleviate suffering and promote the well-being of all beings.

There are examples of the application of Jain principles in peacebuilding and the promotion of social harmony, both historical and contemporary, that illustrate the transformative potential of Ahimsa in conflict resolution. Although Jainism is a minority tradition in many contexts, its ethical principles and non-violent approach have inspired peace movements, social justice initiatives, and peacebuilding efforts in various parts of the world.

Historically, the influence of Jainism on the Indian independence movement led by Mahatma Gandhi is a notable example of the application of Jain principles in the resolution of a large-scale social and political conflict. Gandhi, deeply influenced by Jain philosophy, adopted Satyagraha (truth force), a form of non-violent resistance based on the principles of Ahimsa, truth, and self-sufficiency, as the main strategy to fight against British colonial rule and achieve India's independence. Gandhi's Satyagraha, inspired by Jain Ahimsa, demonstrated the power of non-violence as a transformative force for social and political change, influencing civil rights and peace movements around the world.

Contemporarily, Jain organizations and individuals continue to work actively in promoting peace, non-violence, and social justice in various areas, from community conflict resolution to the defense of human rights and environmental protection. Jain initiatives in interreligious and intercultural dialogue seek to build bridges of understanding and cooperation between different religious and cultural communities, promoting tolerance, mutual respect, and peaceful coexistence. Peace and non-violence education projects are developed in Jain schools and communities, aiming to educate new generations in the values of compassion, empathy, and peaceful conflict resolution. Awareness campaigns on violence and social injustice, inspired by Ahimsa, seek to mobilize public opinion and push for social and political changes that promote peace, justice, and equality.

Jainism as a path to inner peace and world peace offers a holistic and integrated vision of peace, which begins with individual transformation and expands to social and global transformation. Peace, in the Jain perspective, is not only the absence of external conflict, but rather a state of inner harmony, of mental and emotional balance, which arises from the practice of self-discipline, meditation, and karmic purification. Inner peace, cultivated through Jain spiritual practice, radiates to the outside world, positively influencing interpersonal relationships, communities, and society in general.

Jainism teaches us that world peace begins with the inner peace of each individual. By transforming our own hearts and minds, by cultivating compassion, empathy, and non-violence in our daily lives, we can contribute to creating a more peaceful and harmonious world. The practice of Ahimsa, therefore, is not only a personal ethic, but also a strategy for social transformation, a path to building a future of peace and justice for all humanity. Jainism's call for non-violence and peacebuilding resonates with urgency and hope in the contemporary world, offering a beacon of light and a guide to action in times of conflict and uncertainty.

In conclusion, Jainism offers a profound and comprehensive approach to peacebuilding, centered on the principle of Ahimsa as a tool for conflict resolution at all levels. The importance of dialogue, mutual understanding, and empathy is emphasized as essential means to overcome violence. Historical and contemporary examples demonstrate the applicability of Jain principles in promoting social harmony and world peace. Jainism, ultimately, proposes a path of personal and social transformation, where the search for inner peace becomes inseparable from the search for peace in the world, inviting us to act with Ahimsa as agents of positive change and builders of a more peaceful and compassionate future for all beings. In the next chapter, we will explore Jainism and interreligious dialogue, unveiling the Jain perspective on other faiths and its contribution to understanding religious diversity.

Chapter 23
Interreligious Dialogue

In a globalized and plural world, where different religious traditions coexist and interact increasingly, interreligious dialogue emerges as a pressing need for building peace, mutual understanding, and global cooperation. Jainism, with its inclusive and tolerant philosophy, offers a uniquely valuable perspective for this dialogue, based on the principle of Anekantavada (relativism) and a deep ethic of respect and non-violence towards all beliefs and points of view. Exploring Jainism and interreligious dialogue is to unveil the Jain approach to religious diversity, understanding how its principles can contribute to overcoming fanaticism, intolerance, and religious conflict, promoting a spirit of collaboration and the search for universal values among different faith traditions.

Anekantavada as a basis for interreligious dialogue and understanding religious diversity is the cornerstone of the Jain perspective on other faiths. Anekantavada, the doctrine of the multiplicity of perspectives and the relativity of truth, teaches that reality is complex and multifaceted, and that no single perspective can capture it in its entirety. Applied to the religious field, Anekantavada implies that no religion has a monopoly on absolute truth, and that each religious tradition represents a valid and valuable perspective on the nature of ultimate reality, the spiritual path, and the purpose of life.

This pluralistic and inclusive view contrasts with exclusivist religious approaches that affirm the superiority or uniqueness of their own faith, often leading to intolerance, proselytism, and interreligious conflict. Jain Anekantavada, by recognizing the validity and importance of all religious perspectives, promotes a spirit of intellectual humility, tolerance, and respect for other faith traditions. Interreligious dialogue, in the Jain perspective, is not seen as a competition to convert or refute other religions, but rather as an opportunity to learn from each other, to enrich one's own spiritual understanding, and to work together in the search for universal values and solutions to the challenges of humanity.

Jain respect and tolerance for other religious traditions are distinctive features of the Jain stance in interreligious dialogue. Jainism, throughout its history, has demonstrated a remarkable ability to coexist peacefully with other religions in India and other parts of the world, avoiding aggressive proselytism and religious conflict. This respect and tolerance stem directly from the principle of Anekantavada, which encourages Jains to see the truth in all perspectives, even those that differ from their own beliefs.

Jainism does not consider other religions as false or inferior, but rather as different paths that can lead to spiritual realization and the pursuit of good.

Recognizing that different people have different needs, temperaments, and cultural contexts, Jainism accepts that different religions can offer valid and appropriate paths for different individuals. This respect for religious diversity does not imply moral relativism or indifference to truth, but rather a recognition of the complexity of the human spiritual quest and the legitimacy of different approaches to the same ultimate goal.

There are points of convergence and dialogue between Jainism and other religions, such as Buddhism, Hinduism, Christianity, Islam, and other faith traditions, that can be explored to promote mutual understanding and interreligious cooperation. Although each religion has its own specific doctrines, rituals, and practices, there are universal ethical values and principles that are shared by many religious traditions, offering common ground for dialogue and collaboration.

With Buddhism, Jainism shares a common historical and cultural origin in Ancient India, and a series of similar principles and practices, such as the emphasis on non-violence, asceticism, meditation, and the pursuit of liberation from suffering. Jain-Buddhist dialogue can explore the nuances and differences in their doctrines, such as the concept of soul (Jiva in Jainism and Anatta in Buddhism), ascetic practice (more radical in Jainism and the Middle Way in Buddhism), and epistemology (Anekantavada in Jainism and emphasis on emptiness in Buddhism), enriching mutual understanding and identifying areas of ethical and spiritual convergence.

With Hinduism, Jainism shares a vast common cultural and historical ground, and a series of shared concepts and practices, such as belief in Karma, reincarnation, Dharma, and the pursuit of liberation (Moksha). Jain-Hindu dialogue can explore the differences in their views on divinity, the caste system, rituals, and ascetic practices, seeking to identify common ethical and spiritual values and areas of social and environmental collaboration.

With Christianity and Islam, Jain dialogue can explore the points of ethical and spiritual convergence, such as the importance of compassion, justice, peace, love for one's neighbor, and the search for a relationship with the transcendent. Although theological and cosmological doctrines differ significantly, dialogue can focus on shared ethical values, the importance of social action for justice and peace, and the search for common ground for collaboration on issues of global concern, such as poverty, inequality, violence, and the environmental crisis.

The search for universal values and common ethical principles among different religions is an important goal of interreligious dialogue in the Jain perspective. Despite the diversity of religious doctrines, rituals, and practices, many faith traditions share fundamental ethical values, such as compassion, justice, honesty, peace, generosity, respect, and responsibility. These universal values can serve as a basis for interreligious cooperation in areas such as promoting peace, defending human rights, combating poverty and inequality, protecting the environment, and building a more just and compassionate world.

Interreligious dialogue, in the Jain perspective, does not aim to homogenize or dilute the differences between religions, but rather to recognize and value religious diversity as a richness for humanity. The search for universal values does not imply denying or minimizing the particularities of each religious tradition, but rather identifying the common ground that can unite different faiths in the pursuit of a greater good. Jainism, with its inclusive and tolerant philosophy, offers a valuable contribution to this dialogue, inviting different religions to work together in building a more peaceful, just, and harmonious world for all beings.

In conclusion, Jainism and interreligious dialogue meet in the principle of Anekantavada, a philosophy that promotes tolerance, respect, and understanding of religious diversity. Jainism demonstrates a deep respect and tolerance for other faith traditions, seeking points of convergence and dialogue with Buddhism, Hinduism, Christianity, Islam, and other religions. The search for universal values and common ethical principles among different religions is seen as a path to interreligious cooperation and the building of a more peaceful and just world. Jainism, with its inclusive and dialogical perspective, offers a valuable contribution to the contemporary interreligious scene, inviting different faiths to work together in the pursuit of a future of peace, harmony, and mutual understanding for all humanity. In the next chapter, we will explore the presence of Jainism in the diaspora, unveiling the formation of Jain communities outside India and their challenges and adaptations in the modern world.

Chapter 24
Jainism in the Diaspora

On the threshold of the 21st century, Jainism, an ancient religious and philosophical tradition with deep roots in India, has expanded its geographical and cultural boundaries, establishing vibrant and flourishing communities in the diaspora, in various corners of the world. This Jain diaspora, driven by migratory movements and the search for opportunities in different nations, represents a new and dynamic chapter in the history of Jainism, bringing with it challenges and adaptations, but also unique opportunities for the global dissemination of Jain teachings and the enrichment of the multicultural tapestry of the contemporary world. Exploring Jainism in the diaspora is to unveil the journey of an ancestral faith in foreign lands, understanding how the Jain community reinvents and strengthens itself in new cultural contexts, maintaining its identity and contributing to the construction of a more diverse and interconnected world.

The expansion of Jainism outside India in the 20th and 21st centuries marks a turning point in the history of the Jain tradition. For centuries, Jainism remained predominantly confined to the Indian subcontinent, with communities concentrated mainly in India, and to a lesser extent, in some neighboring countries. However, starting in the 20th century, and especially in recent decades, Jainism has witnessed a growing diaspora movement, with Jains migrating to different parts of the world in search of better economic, educational, and professional opportunities.

The factors that drove the Jain diaspora are multiple and complex, reflecting global migration trends and the socioeconomic dynamics of the contemporary world. Globalization, increased international mobility, the search for better living conditions, and the diaspora of other Indian communities were some of the main catalysts for the expansion of Jainism beyond India's borders. The Jain diaspora, while representing a challenge in terms of maintaining cultural and religious identity, also offers unprecedented opportunities for the global dissemination of Jain teachings, interaction with different cultures, and building bridges between East and West.

The formation of Jain communities in North America, Europe, Africa, Asia, and Oceania testifies to the global reach of the Jain diaspora. In North America, the United States and Canada are home to the largest Jain communities in the diaspora, with Jain centers, temples, and community organizations established in various cities, such as New York, Chicago, Los Angeles, Toronto, and Vancouver. In Europe, the United Kingdom, Belgium, Germany, and France are some of the countries with a more significant Jain presence, with communities in cities such as London, Leicester, Antwerp, and Paris. In Africa, Jain communities can be found mainly in Kenya, South Africa, and Uganda, reflecting the historical migration of Indians to the African continent. In Asia, beyond India, Jain communities are present in countries such as Singapore, Malaysia, Thailand, and Japan, often composed of Indian immigrants and their descendants. In Oceania, Australia and New Zealand have also witnessed the formation of Jain communities, mainly in large cities.

These Jain communities in the diaspora, while sharing the same faith and fundamental values, reflect an internal diversity in terms of regional origin, Jain sect (Digambara or Svetambara), language, cultural practices, and degrees of adaptation to the local context. The Jain diaspora is not a monolithic bloc, but rather a mosaic of communities with their own nuances and dynamics.

The challenges and adaptations of Jainism in the diaspora are complex and multifaceted, requiring continuous efforts to maintain cultural and religious identity, transmit values to new generations, and adapt Jain practices to new cultural contexts. One of the main challenges is the maintenance of cultural and religious identity in a cultural and religious environment different from India. The Jain diaspora faces the pressure of cultural assimilation, the difficulty of maintaining Jain traditions in a secularized context, and the need to transmit the Jain faith and culture to new generations, who often grow up in a predominantly non-Jain environment.

To address this challenge, Jain communities in the diaspora have striven to create community centers, temples, and religious organizations that serve as meeting points, places of worship, centers of religious education, and places of cultural preservation. The transmission of values to new generations is a priority, with religious education programs for children and young people, Jainology classes, spiritual retreats, and cultural activities aimed at strengthening Jain identity and connection with tradition.

The adaptation of Jain practices to the context of the diaspora is another important challenge. Some Jain practices, such as temple rituals, rigorous fasts, and specific dietary restrictions, can be difficult to maintain fully in a cultural and social environment different from India. Jain communities in the diaspora have sought to adapt Jain practices in a creative and flexible way, maintaining the essence of Jain principles, but adjusting the forms of practice to make them more accessible and relevant in the context of life in the diaspora. For example, temple rituals can be simplified, fasts can be adapted to health conditions and Western lifestyle, and dietary restrictions can be interpreted more flexibly, always maintaining the commitment to Ahimsa and vegetarianism.

The contribution of the Jain diaspora to the global dissemination of Jain teachings is notable and growing. Jain communities in the diaspora act as cultural and spiritual bridges between Jainism and the Western world, promoting interreligious dialogue, intercultural understanding, and the dissemination of Jain values of peace, non-violence, tolerance, and respect for all life. Jain centers in the diaspora offer lectures, workshops, courses, and publications on Jainism, attracting people from different cultural and religious backgrounds interested in learning about Jain philosophy and ethics.

The Jain diaspora has used new communication and information technologies, such as the internet, social networks, and online platforms, to disseminate Jain teachings globally, reach a wider audience, and promote interreligious and intercultural dialogue on a global scale. Jain organizations in the diaspora have translated Jain scriptures, produced educational materials in various languages, organized international events and conferences, and created online communication networks that connect Jains and those interested in Jainism around the world.

The Jain diaspora, therefore, is not only a migratory phenomenon, but also an agent of transformation and dissemination of Jainism, contributing to the expansion of the influence of the Jain tradition in the contemporary world. Through its efforts to maintain cultural and religious identity, adapt Jain practices, and disseminate Jain teachings globally, the Jain diaspora plays a crucial role in the vitality and continuity of the Jain tradition in the 21st century, ensuring that the ancient wisdom of Jainism continues to inspire and guide people in different parts of the world in the search for an ethical, peaceful, and meaningful life.

In conclusion, Jainism in the diaspora represents a dynamic and multifaceted chapter in the history of the Jain tradition. The expansion of Jainism outside India in the 20th and 21st centuries has resulted in the formation of vibrant Jain communities on various continents, facing challenges of adaptation and maintenance of identity, but also seizing opportunities to disseminate Jain teachings globally. The Jain diaspora, with its community centers, temples, educational programs, and online initiatives, contributes significantly to the vitality and relevance of Jainism in the modern world, acting as a cultural and spiritual bridge and promoting the Jain values of peace, non-violence, and universal harmony. In the next chapter, we will explore the challenges and contemporary issues in Jainism, unveiling the modern adaptations and concerns that the Jain tradition faces in the 21st century.

Chapter 25
Contemporary Challenges

At the threshold of the 21st century, Jainism, like many other religious traditions, navigates a sea of contemporary challenges and issues, inherent to the complexity and rapid transformations of the modern world. Facing the waves of secularism, materialism, globalization, and modernity, Jainism seeks creative and relevant adaptations to maintain its vitality, preserve its core values, and respond to the concerns and questions of its practitioners and society at large. Exploring the contemporary challenges and issues in Jainism means delving into the complexities of the Jain tradition in the modern world, understanding the tensions between tradition and modernity, the internal and external debates, and the efforts to reimagine and revitalize Jainism for the 21st century.

The internal and external challenges faced by Jainism in the modern world are diverse and interconnected, reflecting the cultural, social, and intellectual trends of our time. Among the external challenges, Jainism, like other religions, confronts growing secularism in many parts of the world, where the influence of religion in public and private life diminishes, and secular values such as rationalism, individualism, and materialism gain prominence. Materialism, with its emphasis on material possessions, consumption, and worldly success, challenges Jain values of simplicity, non-possessiveness (Aparigraha), and the pursuit of spiritual values. Globalization, while offering opportunities for the dissemination of Jainism in the diaspora, also exposes the Jain tradition to diverse and sometimes challenging cultural influences, questioning traditional forms of Jain practice and identity.

Among the internal challenges, Jainism, as a living tradition, faces internal debates and tensions over the interpretation and application of Jain principles in the modern world. Issues related to gender, the caste system (although Jainism formally rejects the caste system, vestiges of social hierarchies may persist in some Jain communities), social justice, and human rights are subject to reflection and debate within the Jain community, seeking to adapt Jain values to the ethical and social challenges of the 21st century.

Contemporary issues in Jainism reflect the ethical and social concerns and dilemmas that the Jain tradition faces in the modern world. The issue of gender, for example, is a topic of debate in many religions, including Jainism. Although historical Jainism granted a significant role to women in religious practice and monasticism, some Jain traditions, especially within the Digambara sect, maintain more restrictive views on the role of women in monastic and spiritual life. Contemporary debates within Jainism question the need for greater gender equality in all spheres of Jain life, including access to monasticism, religious leadership, and participation in rituals and practices.

The issue of social justice and Jainism's social engagement in the modern world is also a relevant topic. Although Jainism emphasizes compassion, non-violence, and charity (Dana), some critics argue that the Jain tradition has focused excessively on individual liberation and monastic asceticism, neglecting active engagement in the pursuit of social justice and the resolution of social problems such as poverty, inequality, and oppression. Contemporary debates within Jainism explore the implications of Ahimsa for social and political action, seeking ways to apply Jain principles in promoting social justice, equality, and the defense of human rights, without compromising the principle of non-violence.

Modern adaptations and innovations in the practice and interpretation of Jainism demonstrate the ability of the Jain tradition to reinvent itself and remain relevant in the modern world. Faced with the challenges of secularism and materialism, Jain communities have sought new ways of presenting and experiencing the Jain Dharma, adapting traditional practices and incorporating elements of modern culture to make Jainism more accessible and attractive to new generations.

In the field of practice, there is a trend towards simplification and adaptation of ascetic rituals and practices, seeking to make them more practical and relevant for laypeople living in the secular world. The practice of meditation (Samayika), vegetarianism, and charity (Dana) continue to be emphasized as central practices for Jain laypeople, adapted to modern lifestyles and incorporating elements of contemporary spirituality, such as mindfulness and compassion. Jain education has also been adapting, using new technologies and online platforms to disseminate Jain teachings, reach a wider audience, and create communication and learning networks online for Jains around the world.

In the field of interpretation, there is a trend towards reinterpreting Jain principles in light of the challenges and values of the modern world. The principle of Ahimsa, for example, has been reinterpreted and expanded to encompass contemporary issues such as environmental ethics, animal rights, social justice, and peacebuilding. The principle of Anekantavada is used to promote interreligious and intercultural dialogue, tolerance, and understanding of diversity in the plural and globalized world. Jain philosophy is explored in dialogue with modern scientific thought, seeking to identify points of convergence and mutual insights, and demonstrating the relevance of Jain wisdom to the challenges of the 21st century.

The debate on the relevance and applicability of Jain principles in the 21st century is a reflection of the vitality and self-reflection capacity of the Jain tradition. Some critics question whether Jain principles, with their emphasis on asceticism, renunciation, and radical non-violence, are truly relevant and applicable to the modern world, marked by consumerism, competition, and violence. Others argue that Jain principles, precisely because of their emphasis on non-violence, compassion, simplicity, and the pursuit of spiritual values, are more relevant than ever in the contemporary world, offering an alternative and inspiring path for personal and social transformation, and for the construction of a more peaceful, just, and sustainable future.

The answer to this debate lies in the ability of the Jain community to continue to adapt, reinterpret, and experience Jain principles creatively and relevantly in the modern world. Jainism, as a living tradition, has the capacity to evolve and transform, maintaining its core values, but also responding to the challenges and needs of each era. The vitality of Jainism in the 21st century will depend on its ability to dialogue with the modern world, to respond to contemporary issues, and to continue to inspire people in the pursuit of an ethical, meaningful life in harmony with all beings.

In conclusion, the contemporary challenges and issues in Jainism reflect the creative tension between tradition and modernity, and the ongoing search of the Jain community for relevance and vitality in the 21st century. Issues of gender, social justice, and adaptation of practices are subject to internal debate and reflection. Modern adaptations and innovations in the practice and interpretation of Jainism demonstrate the tradition's ability to reinvent itself. The debate on the relevance and applicability of Jain principles in the modern world stimulates self-reflection and the search for a living and dynamic Jainism for the future. In the next and final chapter, we will explore the future of Jainism, analyzing the perspectives and relevance of the Jain tradition in the

21st century and its potential to contribute to a more ethical, peaceful, and sustainable world.

Chapter 26
The Future of Jainism

As we contemplate the future of Jainism in the 21st century, we are invited to reflect on the enduring relevance of an ancient tradition in a constantly changing world. Jainism, with its profound ethical principles, its inclusive philosophy, and its emphasis on the pursuit of inner peace and universal harmony, has undeniable potential to contribute significantly to a more ethical, peaceful, and sustainable future for humanity and the planet.

To explore the future of Jainism is to contemplate the promising prospects of a living and dynamic tradition that, even while facing contemporary challenges, continues to inspire and guide people in the search for a more meaningful, compassionate life in harmony with all beings.

The potential of Jainism to contribute to a more ethical, peaceful, and sustainable world lies in the essence of its core principles and values. In a world marked by increasing ethical complexity, the persistence of conflict and violence, and the urgency of the environmental crisis, Jainism offers a moral and spiritual guide of remarkable relevance for building a better future.

The Jain ethic of Ahimsa (Non-Violence), with its universal reach and its encompassing of all forms of life, offers a solid foundation for a global ethic that transcends cultural, religious, and national boundaries. Ahimsa, as a fundamental principle of action and conduct, can inspire a profound ethical transformation in various areas of human life, from interpersonal relationships and family life to politics, economics, and science. In a world that cries out for peace, justice, and compassion, the Jain ethic of Ahimsa offers a concrete path for building a more humane and harmonious society.

The Jain philosophy of Anekantavada (Relativism), with its emphasis on the multiplicity of perspectives and the relativity of truth, offers a powerful antidote to dogmatism, fanaticism, and intolerance, promoting interreligious and intercultural dialogue, mutual understanding, and the peaceful resolution of conflicts. In a world marked by ideological, religious, and cultural divisions, the Jain Anekantavada offers an inclusive and tolerant perspective, which recognizes the validity of different points of view and encourages the search for common ground and collaboration for the common good.

The Jain lifestyle, centered on simplicity, non-possessiveness (Aparigraha), conscious consumption, vegetarianism, and self-discipline, offers a sustainable and compassionate model for the 21st century. In a world confronted with the environmental crisis, the depletion of natural resources, and unbridled consumerism, the Jain lifestyle proposes an ethical and ecological alternative, which prioritizes spiritual well-being over material accumulation, harmony with nature over predatory exploitation, and moderation over excess. The Jain lifestyle, therefore, can inspire a cultural transformation towards a more sustainable, equitable society focused on values deeper than mere material consumption.

The relevance of Jain principles for resolving contemporary global challenges is becoming increasingly evident in a complex and interconnected world. Climate change, loss of biodiversity, pollution, social inequality, violence, interreligious and intercultural conflicts are some of the urgent global challenges that require innovative and transformative solutions. Jain principles offer a valuable ethical and philosophical perspective for addressing these challenges in a holistic and integrated way.

Jain environmental Ahimsa offers a guide for action in the context of the climate crisis and the loss of biodiversity, encouraging the adoption of sustainable practices, the protection of ecosystems, and the pursuit of a harmonious relationship with nature. The principle of non-violence can be applied in conflict resolution and peacebuilding, promoting dialogue, mediation, tolerance, and the search for peaceful solutions to disputes, both at the interpersonal and international levels. The Jain ethic of social justice, based on compassion, equity, and respect for all beings, can inspire the fight against poverty, inequality, and oppression, and the construction of more just and inclusive societies.

The importance of preserving and promoting Jain teachings for future generations lies in the conviction that the ancient wisdom of Jainism has perennial value and continuing relevance for humanity. In a rapidly changing world, where traditional values are often questioned and the search for meaning and purpose intensifies, Jainism offers a solid and coherent spiritual path, based on universal ethical principles and a deep and comprehensive philosophy.

The preservation and promotion of Jain teachings for future generations require continuous and creative efforts by the Jain community and all those who recognize the value of the Jain tradition. Jain education, from childhood to adulthood, is essential to transmit Jain values, sacred scriptures, spiritual practices, and Jain culture to new generations. The use of new communication and information technologies can be harnessed to disseminate Jain teachings globally, reach a wider audience, and create online learning and practice networks. Interreligious and intercultural dialogue is essential to present Jainism to different cultures and to build bridges of understanding and cooperation with other religious and secular traditions.

The future of Jainism as a living and dynamic spiritual tradition depends on the capacity of the Jain community to adapt, reinvent itself, and respond to the challenges and opportunities of the 21st century, maintaining the essence of its principles and values, but also incorporating new forms of expression and practice that make Jainism relevant and attractive to new generations. Jainism, with its long history of resilience, adaptation, and renewal, has the potential to continue to flourish and contribute to the positive transformation of the world, offering a path of inner peace, universal harmony, and the pursuit of spiritual liberation for all those who are inspired by its teachings.

In conclusion, the future of Jainism is promising and relevant in the 21st century. Its potential to contribute to a more ethical, peaceful, and sustainable world is undeniable, especially in the context of contemporary global challenges. The relevance of Jain principles for resolving these challenges is increasingly recognized. The importance of preserving and promoting Jain teachings for future generations is crucial to ensure the continuity of the tradition and its contribution to a better world. Jainism, as a living and dynamic spiritual tradition, has a bright future ahead, inviting us to reflect on its values, practice its principles, and build together a future of peace, compassion, and harmony for all humanity and the planet.

In the next and final chapter, we will make a comparative analysis between Jainism and Buddhism, exploring the similarities and differences between these two spiritual traditions originating in Ancient India.

Chapter 27
Similarities with Buddhism

In the rich panorama of ancient India's spiritual traditions, Jainism and Buddhism emerge as two distinct yet interconnected currents of thought, sharing historical roots, ethical values, and spiritual goals, while diverging in philosophical doctrines, ascetic practices, and approaches to liberation. A comparative analysis of Jainism and Buddhism reveals a fascinating landscape of similarities and differences, enriching our understanding of both traditions and illuminating the nuances of the human spiritual quest. Exploring the similarities and differences between Jainism and Buddhism is to enter a millenary dialogue between two of India's most important spiritual traditions, unveiling their convergences and divergences, and appreciating the richness and complexity of their legacies.

A comparative analysis of the origins, doctrines, and practices of Jainism and Buddhism reveals a panorama of convergences and divergences that reflect their historical trajectories and their distinct approaches to the spiritual quest. Both traditions emerged in ancient India in the 6th century BC, during a period of intense religious and philosophical effervescence, known as the Shramana period, which questioned the Vedic religious traditions and sought alternative paths to liberation from suffering. Both Mahavira, the last Tirthankara of Jainism, and Siddhartha Gautama, the Buddha, were historical figures who renounced worldly life, practiced asceticism, and attained enlightenment, becoming the founders of their respective traditions.

Among the points of convergence between Jainism and Buddhism, the following stand out:

Emphasis on Non-Violence (Ahimsa): Both Jainism and Buddhism place non-violence (Ahimsa) at the center of their ethics and spiritual practice. Both traditions condemn violence in all its forms and advocate compassion, benevolence, and respect for all living beings as paths to inner peace and universal harmony.

Asceticism: Both Jainism and Buddhism value asceticism as a means of karmic purification, self-discipline, and the pursuit of liberation. Both traditions encourage renunciation of sensory pleasures, detachment from material possessions, and the practice of austerities such as fasting, meditation, and silence, as ways to strengthen the mind and spirit.

Rejection of the Caste System: Both Jainism and Buddhism, in their origins, rejected the hierarchical caste system of Vedic society, advocating the spiritual equality of all human beings, regardless of their social origin or caste. Both traditions opened their doors to people of all castes, including those considered "untouchable" in Vedic society, promoting a more egalitarian and inclusive vision of the religious community.

Quest for Liberation (Moksha/Nirvana): Both Jainism and Buddhism share the ultimate goal of liberation from the cycle of birth and death (Samsara) and suffering (Dukha). Although the nomenclatures and descriptions of the state of liberation (Moksha in Jainism and Nirvana in Buddhism) may vary, both traditions seek a state of infinite peace, bliss, and freedom from the limitations of conditioned existence.

Despite the significant similarities, Jainism and Buddhism also present significant divergences in their philosophical doctrines, ascetic practices, and approaches to liberation, reflecting their distinct historical trajectories and their particular emphases.

Among the significant divergences, the following stand out:

Concept of Soul (Jiva/Anatta): One of the most fundamental doctrinal differences between Jainism and Buddhism lies in the concept of the soul. Jainism postulates the existence of Jiva, an individual, conscious, eternal, and inherently pure soul, present in all living beings. Buddhism, in turn, adopts the doctrine of Anatta (no-self), denying the existence of a permanent, immutable, and substantial soul, arguing that the human personality is a dynamic flow of physical and mental processes, without a permanent or substantial core. This difference in the concept of the soul has significant implications for the cosmology, ethics, and soteriology of both traditions.

Radical Asceticism (Jainism) vs. Middle Way (Buddhism): While both traditions value asceticism, Jainism adopts a radical asceticism, seeking karmic purification and liberation through extremely austere practices, such as prolonged fasting, rigorous food restriction, monastic nudity (in the Digambara tradition), and the practice of Ahimsa in its most extreme form, avoiding harming any form of life, even microorganisms. Buddhism, in turn, adopts the Middle Way, seeking a balance between extreme asceticism and sensual indulgence, advocating a moderate path of spiritual practice that avoids extremes and promotes the harmonious development of the body, mind, and spirit.

Anekantavada (Jainism) vs. Emphasis on Emptiness (Buddhism): In the epistemological and philosophical field, Jainism developed the doctrine of Anekantavada (relativism), which emphasizes the multiplicity of perspectives and the relativity of truth, arguing that reality is complex and multifaceted, and that no single perspective can capture it completely. Buddhism, in turn, emphasizes the emptiness (Sunyata) of all phenomena, arguing that all phenomena are empty of inherent, substantial, and permanent existence, and that understanding emptiness is essential for liberation from suffering. Although both doctrines recognize the complexity and illusory nature of conditioned reality, they differ in their emphases and in their implications for spiritual practice and the understanding of ultimate truth.

The mutual influence and historical coexistence of Jainism and Buddhism in India attest to the proximity and interaction between these two traditions over the centuries. Although they have developed as distinct traditions with their own doctrines and practices,

Jainism and Buddhism coexisted peacefully in India for many centuries, influencing each other in various aspects. There is evidence of philosophical dialogue and exchange of ideas between Jain and Buddhist thinkers, as well as mutual influence in ascetic practices, rituals, and forms of artistic expression. Despite their doctrinal differences, Jainism and Buddhism share a common ethical and spiritual ground, promoting non-violence, compassion, self-discipline, and the pursuit of liberation from suffering, and contributing significantly to the rich spiritual tapestry of India.

In conclusion, Jainism and Buddhism, although distinct in their doctrines and practices, share important similarities in their origins, ethical values, and spiritual goals. Both traditions emphasize non-violence, asceticism, the rejection of the caste system, and the pursuit of liberation. However, they diverge significantly in their concepts of soul, ascetic approaches, and philosophical emphases, with Jainism adopting a more radical asceticism and a relativistic epistemology (Anekantavada), while Buddhism emphasizes the Middle Way and the doctrine of emptiness (Anatta and Sunyata). Despite their differences, Jainism and Buddhism coexisted peacefully in India for centuries, influencing each other and contributing valuably to the spiritual heritage of humanity. In the next and penultimate chapter, we will explore the lasting legacy of Jainism and its impact on Indian and global thought.

Chapter 28
The Enduring Legacy of Jainism

Jainism, although sometimes less visible on the world religious stage than other Indian traditions such as Hinduism and Buddhism, has left a lasting and profound impact on Indian and global thought, reverberating through the centuries and influencing various aspects of culture, ethics, philosophy, and spiritual practices. This multifaceted and subtle legacy manifests itself not only in Jain communities around the world, but also in values, movements, and ideas that have shaped and continue to shape the intellectual and moral landscape of humanity. Exploring the enduring legacy of Jainism is to unravel the persistence and relevance of an ancient wisdom, understanding how its principles and values continue to inspire and guide individuals and societies in the pursuit of a more ethical, peaceful, and harmonious world.

Jainism's influence on Indian ethics and philosophy is undeniable and seminal, permeating the ethical and philosophical thought of India over millennia. The fundamental principle of Ahimsa (Non-Violence), the cornerstone of Jain ethics, has become a central value in Indian culture, influencing not only other religious traditions, such as Hinduism and

Buddhism, but also social, political, and philosophical movements throughout Indian history. Jain Ahimsa, in its breadth and depth, goes beyond mere abstention from physical violence, incorporating verbal, mental, and emotional non-violence, and extending to all forms of life, profoundly influencing the Indian ideal of respect for all living beings.

The doctrine of Anekantavada (Relativism), the Jain philosophy of the multiplicity of perspectives and the relativity of truth, has also left an indelible mark on Indian philosophical thought, promoting tolerance, dialogue, and understanding of the diversity of viewpoints. Anekantavada, by recognizing the complexity of reality and the limitation of individual perspective, encouraged the development of more inclusive and dialogical philosophical approaches, influencing intellectual debate and the search for truth in India over the centuries. Jain ethics, centered on Ahimsa, and Jain epistemology, based on Anekantavada, constitute unique and lasting philosophical contributions to the intellectual heritage of India and the world.

Jainism's contribution to the development of vegetarianism and the animal rights movement is notable and pioneering, making Jainism one of the oldest and most consistent religious traditions advocating vegetarianism and animal ethics. The principle of Ahimsa, with its extension to all forms of life, led Jainism to adopt a strict vegetarianism as an essential practice, avoiding the consumption of meat, fish, eggs, and ideally dairy products, to minimize violence against animals and reduce suffering in the world. Jainism not only advocates vegetarianism as a personal practice, but also promotes it as an ethical and social ideal, influencing the development of vegetarianism in India and, more recently, contributing to the growth of the vegetarian and vegan movement on a global scale.

Jainism, with its emphasis on compassion for all living beings and the rejection of violence in all its forms, has played a crucial role in shaping the animal rights movement, anticipating concepts and arguments that would become central to the contemporary debate on animal rights. The Jain view that animals have souls, the capacity to feel pain and suffering, and the right to life and well-being, resonates with the ethical concerns of the animal rights movement, and continues to inspire activists and thinkers in the struggle for the protection and liberation of animals.

The impact of Jainism on Indian art, architecture, and literature is evident in majestic temples, serene sculptures, intricate paintings, and rich and diverse scriptures. The architecture of Jain temples, such as the Derasars of Ranakpur, Mount Abu, and Khajuraho, represents a remarkable artistic legacy, characterized by beauty, complexity, and harmony, reflecting the Jain values of peace, serenity, and the pursuit of transcendence. The sculptures of the Tirthankaras, with their serene and contemplative expressions, have become icons of Jain art, conveying a message of inner peace and spiritual perfection. Jain paintings, especially the miniatures of illuminated manuscripts, stand out for their precision, detail, and symbolic richness, narrating religious stories, representing cosmological diagrams, and conveying the teachings of the Jain Dharma.

Jain literature, encompassing the Agamas, Puranas, Charitas, and various other works, constitutes a vast and rich corpus of philosophical, ethical, narrative, poetic, and grammatical texts, preserved in ancient languages such as Ardhamagadhi, Sanskrit, and Apabhramsa. This literature offers a treasure trove of spiritual wisdom, philosophical insights, inspiring narratives, and examples of ethical living, contributing significantly to India's literary heritage and to the understanding of the Jain tradition.

The legacy of Jainism as a tradition of peace, non-violence, and spiritual seeking transcends specific contributions in ethics, philosophy, vegetarianism, and art, encompassing the essence of the Jain tradition itself and its fundamental message to humanity. Jainism, throughout its history, has stood as a beacon of peace and non-violence, advocating for the peaceful resolution of conflicts, religious tolerance, and the pursuit of a more harmonious and compassionate world. The Jain emphasis on individual spiritual seeking, self-discipline, meditation, and karmic purification offers a path to inner transformation and the realization of human potential for spiritual perfection and liberation from suffering.

Jainism, in its essence, invites reflection on the nature of existence, the purpose of life, and the path to happiness and liberation. Its enduring legacy lies in the transmission of eternal values, such as non-violence, compassion, honesty, non-possessiveness, and the pursuit of truth, which continue to inspire and guide people in different parts of the world in the search for a more ethical, meaningful life in harmony with all beings.

The relevance of Jainism to contemporary ethical and spiritual thought is notable and growing in a world confronted with complex and urgent challenges. In a time of violence, conflict, inequality, social injustice, and environmental crisis, Jain wisdom offers a valuable ethical and spiritual counterpoint, proposing an alternative path based on non-violence, compassion, sustainability, and the pursuit of inner peace. Jainism, with its message of respect for all forms of life, its ethics of individual responsibility, and its vision of an interconnected world, resonates with the concerns and aspirations of the 21st century.

The enduring legacy of Jainism, therefore, is not only a historical heritage, but also a source of inspiration and guidance for the future. Its principles and values continue to challenge and enrich contemporary ethical and spiritual thought, offering a path for personal and social transformation, and for the construction of a more peaceful, just, and harmonious world for all living beings.

In conclusion, the enduring legacy of Jainism is multifaceted and profound, radiating its impact on Indian and global thought through ethics, philosophy, vegetarianism, the animal rights movement, art, architecture, literature, and its core message of peace, non-violence, and spiritual seeking. Jainism, as a tradition of ancient wisdom, continues to offer a valuable contribution to contemporary ethical and spiritual thought, remaining relevant and inspiring for the 21st century and for future generations. In the next and final chapter, we will synthesize the main teachings and values of Jainism, reflecting on its potential as a path to inner peace and universal harmony.

Chapter 29
A Path to Inner Peace

As we reach the end of this exploration of the rich and multifaceted Jain tradition, it is opportue to recap the central teachings and values that permeate each chapter of this book, synthesizing the essence of Jainism and reflecting on its profound potential as a path to inner peace and universal harmony. Jainism, more than a religion in the conventional sense, reveals itself as a comprehensive and transformative philosophy of life, a practical and ethical guide for the human journey towards liberation from suffering and the realization of full spiritual potential. In this concluding chapter, we will revisit the fundamental pillars of Jainism, reiterating its perennial relevance and universal appeal in a world that yearns for peace, compassion, and wisdom.

Revisiting the main teachings and values of Jainism, we can identify a set of interconnected principles that form the core of the Jain tradition. At the center of everything lies Ahimsa (Non-Violence), the supreme and comprehensive principle that permeates all aspects of Jain life, from personal conduct and dietary choices to social engagement and the pursuit of world peace. Jain Ahimsa is not limited to the absence of physical violence, but extends to non-violence in thought, word, and action, and to all forms of life, recognizing the interconnectedness and sacredness of all living beings.

Intertwined with Ahimsa is the principle of Anekantavada (Relativism), the Jain philosophy of the multiplicity of perspectives and the relativity of truth. Anekantavada promotes tolerance, intellectual humility, and dialogue, recognizing that no single perspective can capture the complexity of reality, and that truth can be approached from different angles and from different points of view. This inclusive and pluralistic view is fundamental to interreligious dialogue, intercultural understanding, and the peaceful resolution of conflicts.

The Tri-Ratna (Three Jewels) of Jainism - Samyak Darshan (Right View), Samyak Jnana (Right Knowledge), and Samyak Charitra (Right Conduct) - represent the Jain path to liberation (Moksha). Right View implies having faith in the teachings of the Tirthankaras and in the possibility of liberation. Right Knowledge involves understanding Jain doctrines, cosmology, ethics, and spiritual practices. Right Conduct refers to the practice of the Five Great Vows (Mahavratas) for monks and nuns, and the Five Lesser Vows (Anuvratas) for laymen and laywomen, guiding ethical and moral conduct in everyday life.

The Five Great Vows (Mahavratas) - Ahimsa (Non-Violence), Satya (Truth), Asteya (Non-Stealing), Brahmacharya (Celibacy/Chastity), and Aparigraha (Non-Possessiveness) - represent the fundamental ethical principles of Jain monastic life, guiding ascetics in the pursuit of karmic purification and liberation. The Five Lesser Vows (Anuvratas), adapted for laymen and laywomen, offer an ethical guide for everyday life, encouraging the practice of non-violence, truth, honesty, fidelity, and moderation in consumption.

Ascetic practice and spiritual discipline are central to Jainism, aiming at the purification of Karma, the control of the senses, and the pursuit of liberation. Fasting, meditation, prayer, the study of scriptures, and the practice of virtue are some of the Jain spiritual practices that aid in the journey towards Moksha. Compassion (Karuna) and universal friendship (Maitri) are essential values in Jainism, inspiring altruistic action, charity (Dana), and the pursuit of the well-being of all living beings.

The potential of Jainism as a path to inner peace lies in its emphasis on self-discipline, meditation, and mental and emotional purification. Jain practice invites introspection, observation of the mind, and inner transformation, seeking the eradication of passions, attachments, and ignorance, which are the roots of suffering. Jain meditation (Samayika) aims to calm the mind, cultivate mindfulness, and develop concentration, leading to a state of inner peace, mental clarity, and emotional balance.

Jainism as a path to universal harmony manifests itself in its ethics of non-violence extended to all beings, in its inclusive and tolerant philosophy, and in its call to compassion and interconnectedness. The Jain vision of a harmonious world is based on the recognition of the unity of life, the importance of mutual respect, and the need to build a just, peaceful, and sustainable society for all living beings. The practice of Ahimsa, Anekantavada, and Jain values in everyday life can contribute to the creation of a more compassionate, tolerant world in harmony with nature.

In conclusion, Jainism offers a profound and comprehensive path to inner peace and universal harmony, based on universal ethical principles, an inclusive and tolerant philosophy, and transformative spiritual practices. The message of Jainism, with its emphasis on non-violence, compassion, self-discipline, and the pursuit of liberation, resonates with urgency and relevance in the contemporary world, offering a valuable guide for the human journey towards a more peaceful, just, and harmonious future for all living beings. May the wisdom of Jainism continue to inspire and guide individuals and societies in the search for a better world, guided by the light of Ahimsa and universal compassion.

Epilogue

As you reach the end of this reading, something within you, even if subtly, is no longer the same. The words traversed throughout these pages are not mere abstract ideas; they carry the essence of a tradition that challenges our worldview, our daily choices, and, above all, our relationship with existence. Jainism, with its absolute devotion to non-violence, its reverence for truth, and its tireless pursuit of liberation, is not just a distant philosophy, practiced by monks in contemplative silence. It is, and always has been, an invitation to inner transformation – a call to live with more awareness, more responsibility, and more compassion.

The journey we have taken together has revealed a universe of profound and often counterintuitive ideas for the modern mentality. We were introduced to Ahimsa, not just as an ethical principle, but as a non-negotiable commitment to life. We understood that every thought, every word, every action shapes the quality of our soul and determines the course of our karmic journey. We learned that truth is never one-dimensional, but multifaceted, requiring humility and discernment from us. We discovered that liberation is not a gift granted by an external deity, but a state conquered through self-discipline, renunciation, and knowledge.

And now? What remains for the reader who has traveled this path of discovery and contemplation?

Choice remains.

Knowledge alone is not enough. It needs to be lived, experienced, absorbed as part of our essence. Each of us carries an invisible burden, a baggage of thoughts and habits accumulated over countless cycles of existence. Jainism teaches us that this weight can be dissolved, but not by external forces – only by the conscious decision to tread a different path.

Liberation is not a distant concept. It is present in every moment we choose compassion instead of cruelty, silence instead of the thoughtless word, detachment instead of greed. It manifests itself in small choices, in the way we relate to others, in what we consume, in what we cultivate within ourselves.

If there is one thing that Jainism teaches us undeniably, it is that we are solely responsible for our own journey. There are no excuses, no shortcuts. The world around us may be chaotic, violent, indifferent – but our response to it is a choice. Destiny is not imposed on us; it is woven by our own hands, stitched with every thought, every action, every intention.

So, what will you do now?

Perhaps this book has been just an enriching read, a glimpse of a fascinating tradition. Perhaps it has planted a seed that, in due time, will germinate and grow into new understandings. Or perhaps, just perhaps, it has been the beginning of something greater – an awakening, a silent call that will echo in your thoughts long after the last page.

Jainism does not require conversions, does not impose absolute truths, does not seek blind followers. It only offers a path. It is up to each individual to decide whether to follow it, and to what extent they are willing to commit to their own evolution.

If this book has managed to provoke questions, if it has awakened in you a new perspective on life and your own role in the universe, then its mission has been fulfilled.

And now, the next step is yours.

www.ingramcontent.com/pod-product-compliance
Lightning Source LLC
LaVergne TN
LVHW041942070526
838199LV00051BA/2882